Atlanta's
Westview Cemetery

By John Soward Bayne

Gravely Concerned: Southern Writers' Graves

Atlanta's
Westview Cemetery

John Soward Bayne

Afterword by
Franklin Miller Garrett (1906-2000)

Vanity Press
Atlanta
2014

First Edition
5 4 3 2

The Vanity Press logo depicts the seal of Johann Sebastian Bach.
Map on rear cover copyright © 2014 by Weronica Cichosz and Tim Nichols.
Credited photographs copyright © 2014 by the photographers.
Afterword by Franklin Miller Garrett reprinted with permission of
Westview Cemetery, Inc. and the Kenan Research Center of the Atlanta History Center.

Acknowledgments

The following contributed to this project: Sharon Foster Jones, Annie Kinnett Nichols, Tim Nichols, Traci Rylands, Weronica Cichosz, Cooper Starr, Brian Ellison, Owen Talley, Charles Bowen, Jr., Charles Bowen, Sr., Martha Powers, Grant Myers, Susan Olsen, Rodney Mims Cook, Jr., Cheryl Bryan, Wini Hemphill, D. L. Henderson, Cliff Kuhn, Gretchen MacLaughlin, Rebecca Burns, Anne Uhry Abrams, Richard Funderburke, Jen Keith, Elliott Schwalb, Filiberto Hutardo, Mira Hale, Karen Clydesdale, Donna McDaniel, Cindy Julian, Allie Rivenbark, Kay Powell, Coleman Hutchison, Michael McGhee, Sam Wagstaff, David Naugle, Asa Candler VI, Kayla Barrett, Cash Barnes, Paul Hammock, Boyd Coons, Michael Rose, Andy DeLoach, Mark Lulkin, Courtney Lulkin, Christian Moreno, Jada Harris, Paul Crater, Gary Adams, Robert Parks, and Joan Pritchard. My brother Bill visited Atlanta in the wake of the January 2014 ice storm to take pictures. Jeff Clemmons corrected some errors.

I am grateful for the inspiration and camaraderie of the Cemetery and Gravemarkers area of the American Culture Association, especially the chairman, Joe Edgette, and June Hadden Hobbs, who introduced me to this diverse and gracious group of scholars more than a decade ago. My brother Harry and I took a memorable 2006 ACA tour of Westview with the late Helen Sclair, the Cemetery Lady of Chicago. Harry also provided a final edit. And a post-final edit, too.

This being Vanity Press, the author takes responsibility for any errors. With self-publishing and print-on-demand, corrections are relatively easy to effect. The printing services of Lulu seem fine so far. Lulu is also my sister's nickname, and the subject of my master's thesis, the Alban Berg opera.

Carvings on the Abbey loggia feature a Phoenix, the symbol of Atlanta.

Contents

Introduction

> When this you see, remember me.
> - Gertrude Stein, *Four Saints in Three Acts*

Atlanta's Westview Cemetery is a cultural and historical guide to Atlanta's "second cemetery." Established as West View Cemetery in 1884, it is the largest cemetery in the Southeast, 582[1] acres. 106,439[2] people have been interred there during the first 130 years of operation, and there's room for many more.

The founders were Atlanta businessmen, led by Edgar Poe McBurney, faced with there being no more room at Oakland Cemetery, founded in 1850, and wanting to make a grand statement. Their model was Woodlawn in the Bronx in New York City, then as now a glamorous address for the dead.[3]

Westview was built on the site of the Battle of Ezra Church, 28 July 1864, a bloody component of the months-long Atlanta Campaign, which ended with the burning of Atlanta that November.

Westview contains traces of Confederate earthworks from the Civil War, and its water tower, entrance gate, and receiving vault are some of the oldest buildings within the Atlanta city limits. It includes a section dedicated to Confederate veterans, with a monument erected by the Confederate Veterans' Association, with 360 graves.

The Abbey, begun 1943, is one of the largest public mausoleums in the country, built by Cecil Eldridge Bryan (1878-1951), and designed by mausoleum architect Clarence Lee Jay (1888-1983). With space for 11,400 burials[4] the Abbey was the brainchild of Asa Griggs Candler, Jr. (1880-1953), son of the founder of Coca-Cola. Candler owned Westview from 1933 to 1951. An eccentric millionaire, he also created Candler Field, Atlanta's first airport, now Atlanta Hartsfield-Jackson International Airport. For the Abbey, Candler and Bryan pulled out all the stops, with stained-glass windows, a pipe organ, and elaborate stonework.

Candler also introduced some landscaping innovations, removing family-placed shrubbery and other plantings, and requiring flat bronze markers instead of upright monuments in newly developed sections of the cemetery. This practice was in accordance with the latest cemetery style of the memorial park, famously espoused by Hubert Eaton, the founder of Forest Lawn Memorial Park in Glendale, California. When markers are flush with the ground, maintenance is simplified, and graves can be placed closer together. For the cemetery visitor, this is unfortunate; one misses the individuality of a custom grave marker, and must rely on a staff member to locate a grave based on specific landscape features and an index.

---

[1] . . . or 572, or 575, or 577—sources differ. It's big.

[2] As of 6 October 2014. The first burial was 9 October 1884.

[3] Woodlawn boasts of its collection of over 1300 private mausoleums. In 2014 it was the subject of an exhibition at Columbia University's Avery Fine Arts and Architectural Library. Famous burials include Herman Melville, J. C. Penney, Miles Davis, Fiorello LaGuardia, and George M. Cohan.

[4] . . . or 11,444. It's big. A promotional brochure c. 1943 announced a capacity of 5,000; even at that size, it would have been the largest of Bryan's 80 mausoleums.

As at Forest Lawn, some sections of Westview bear names, such as Garden of Gethsemane, Last Supper, Trinity, Good Shepherd, and so on, each with an associated marble sculpture. One section, Acacia Lawn, boasts a masonic sculpture. Near the Abbey are a now-defunct fountain, the site of a former lake called Lake Palmyra, now filled in, and other hardscape elements.

Another feature of the memorial park is comprehensive service:, meaning that mortuary services, flowers, and catering would be available for mourners, all from the cemetery. A funeral home and crematory were planned for Westview, but never realized. During construction of the facility, the Georgia legislature passed a law making it illegal to run a mortuary inside a cemetery. But a florist and greenhouse? Yes. The largest greenhouse in the South, of course, plus a trophy room to display the spoils of Candler's big-game hunts, and a cafeteria for cemetery employees. The greenhouses, trophy room, and cafeteria, all trappings of the Candler period, have now been torn down.

By the late 1940s, some families were complaining about Candler's "improvements," flattening graves and removing shrubs and mounds, and then suing, calling his efforts to recast the landscape in the modern style "desecration." He sold the cemetery in 1951.

The cemetery has been operated as a non-profit company since 1952, when it was purchased from Candler by five men led by Frank Coll Bowen. The cemetery has been managed by the Bowen family ever since, that is, for over half its existence. Other longtime employees include Martha Powers, who has worked there since 1945, when she was hired by Florence Candler, and Grant Myers, whose father formerly worked at Westview, too.

The history of the cemetery is thus conveniently divided into three periods, the McBurney era from 1884, a three-and-a-half-year interregnum when it was owned by members of the Adair family, followed by the Candler era from 1933 to 1951, followed by the Bowen era, since 1952.

Many Adairs and Candlers are buried at Westview, plus other Coca-Cola executives, mayors of Atlanta, a governor of Georgia, writers, a U. S. senator, the former owner of the Atlanta Falcons, religious leaders, and other notables. Their lives and accomplishments tell the story of Atlanta from the waning days of Reconstruction, and include Lost Cause laments, the promise of a New South, numerous wars, the Civil Rights movement, and hip-hop.

Whereas Oakland Cemetery is today a popular public space, with a lively gift shop, regular tours, and annual events, Westview is more of a sleeping giant in Southwest Atlanta. Many Atlantans don't even know it's there. It is dignified and somber.

Among many splendid trees are two Atlanta champions, a Catalpa and a Ginkgo, as well as the original Burfordi holly.

Monuments in Westview include Gothic, Classical, Deco, Egyptian revival, and Eclectic styles. The prevalent late 19th- and 20th-century cemetery landscape trends of the lawn-park cemetery, with upright family markers surrounded by small individual gravestones, and the memorial park cemetery with flush markers, are represented.

Westview, by the way, was the first cemetery in the Southeast to install flush bronze markers.[5]

Available only to whites for much of its history, Westview was integrated as a result of the Civil Rights Act of 1964. Since then, Westview has been a choice burial place for many prominent African Americans, including Donald Lee Hollowell and Vivian Malone Jones. Rapper Chris Kelly is buried there too.

The organization of *Atlanta's Westview Cemetery* is chronological, with photographs of the monuments placed in death-year order. Unless otherwise credited, the photographs are by the author. The intent is for the biographies, uniformly spread over 130 years of Westview's history, to form a historical narrative, through telling the life stories and accomplishments of the memorialized.

The cemetery's entrance faces what was known as Lickskillet Road in Civil War times, then Green's Ferry Road, then Gordon Street, and is now Ralph David Abernathy Boulevard. The northern border, formerly Hunter Street, is now Martin Luther King, Jr. Drive.

Half of the people buried at Westview are women. So this retelling of Atlanta's history has sought to feature notable women, and to include their names. The courtly practice— cultural onomastics—of naming women in the style Mrs. John Soward Bayne in print made it challenging to find women's biographies to include, and so women represent only about 25% of the total.

The second cemetery doesn't house some early Atlanta families, who owned Oakland lots and continued to be buried there long after Westview opened. Famously the author Margaret Mitchell and the golfer Bobby Jones are interred at Oakland, and so are Ansleys, Hurts, Peterses, Rawsons, and Woodwards. There is no Jewish section at Westview, but there are areas designated for Confederate veterans, the Salvation Army, the Sisters of Mercy, the Dominican Sisters, and the Marist Fathers.

Two famous individuals, educator Benjamin Elijah Mays and mayor Ivan Allen, Jr., were formerly interred at Westview but were moved, Mays to the Morehouse College campus and Allen to Oakland. Ivan Allen, Sr., and Ivan Allen III, are both buried at Westview.

The cemetery is so large that visitors go there most successfully by car. The West Lake MARTA station is a fifteen-minute walk to the entrance, with no sidewalks on the cemetery side of Ralph David Abernathy Boulevard. From the entrance gate to the McBurney obelisk is half a mile, and the Abbey is a another half a mile farther still. Note that the streetcar was extended to Westview a few years after it opened. Hardier pilgrims then.

Most typical are "estate lots," wherein a family is buried together, with one large monument bearing the surname, and small headstones or footstones around that. There is no fencing or coping dividing the family lots, or shrubbery.[6] Evidently some sections of the

---

[5] Memorial Park in Memphis also claims to be the first in the Southeast to adopt this style.

[6] Curbs, fences, and shrubbery to delineate lots were forbidden from the earliest days of the cemetery. This was a stylistic innovation of the "lawn park" cemetery. This style succeeded the "rural" or "garden" cemetery movement, of which Oakland is cited as an exemplar. In fact, Oakland is more of a hybrid of the garden cemetery and a "city cemetery," laid out in a grid (its original six acres).

cemetery were intended for single graves (Section 8), two-person lots, and larger ones. There are a number of private mausoleums, and two are particularly interesting, those of Henry Grady and J. J. Haverty. Several of the private mausoleums house deceased Roma people, known for their elaborate mourning and memorializing practices. Some of their interiors are furnished with chairs, vases, dolls, figurines, and other items, giving evidence that the buildings are visited and decorated by surviving family members.

The current (2014) management of the cemetery consists of Charles E. Bowen, Jr., President; Charles E. Bowen, Sr., Vice President; and Martha M. Powers, Secretary.

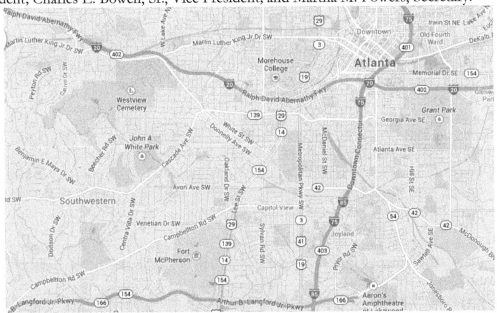

Google map showing cemeteries, 2013. Westview Cemetery is marked in the upper left. Oakland Cemetery is just above the Memorial Drive label, upper right. South-View Cemetery is the boot-shaped area on Jonesboro Road, lower right. Ralph David Abernathy Boulevard is not identified, but it's marked 139 and 29, effectively joining Westview to Grant Park. At Turner Field, just east of the Rodney Cook Downtown Connector, the name changes to Georgia Avenue.

Before Westview

The story of the establishment of Terminus, the end of the railroad line, renamed Marthasville to honor the governor's daughter, then renamed Atlanta, is familiar. An early burial ground near Peachtree and Harris Streets was closed in 1850.

Atlanta's oldest public cemetery, begun in 1850 as a six-acre burial ground known as City Cemetery, expanded to its current 48 acres and was renamed Oakland after the Civil War. The expansion was necessary in part because of the death toll of the war. Approximately 7,000 Confederate dead are buried there, most in unmarked graves, and 16 Union soldiers. Whereas the "original six acres" are laid out in a grid pattern, other parts of the cemetery show the influence of the rural cemetery movement, begun at Mount Auburn in Cambridge, Massachusetts, in 1831. The rural cemetery movement traced its roots to Père LaChaise in Paris, founded in 1804. Features of rural or garden cemeteries include curving lanes, water features, and landscaping; the cemetery was to be regarded as a welcoming public space—the precursor to the public park—where visitors could enjoy nature, picnic, admire the monuments, and reflect on the lives of the memorialized.

By 1880, owing to the growth of the city, all the lots at Oakland had been sold; people who had purchased spaces could still be buried there, but for new applicants the cemetery was effectively closed.

Oakland Cemetery, 1850. Oakland features sections devoted to Confederate war dead, Jews, African Americans, and indigents. The "Black Section" replaces a former "Slave Square" in the original six acres; as the cemetery began to fill up in the 19th century, the real estate became appealing to whites, and the bodies of African Americans were relocated. Notable burials at Oakland include mayors, governors, generals, author Margaret Mitchell, golfer Bobby Jones, and official Atlanta historian Franklin Miller Garrett.

Charner Humphries, 1795-1855, Section 5. Humphries operated the Whitehall Tavern in the West End, predating Atlanta. He was buried in a family cemetery; all the bodies from that cemetery were moved to Westview in 1890. Photograph by Traci Rylands.

Meredith Collier, 1782-1863, Section 4. The patriarch of the Collier family, memorialized in Collier Road, Collier Heights, and other place names, Collier's body was translated to Westview from a church cemetery when his son George Washington Collier died in 1903.

Earthworks near Section 70, 1864. Westview contains traces of Confederate breastworks—so called because armies dug trenches, and mounded dirt chest-high in front to defend their position—from the Battle of Ezra Church. Photograph by William Candler Bayne.

Ezra Church Monument. Westview Cemetery is the site of the Battle of Ezra Church, 28 July 1864, a week after the Battle of Atlanta. The city was under siege until 15 November when the city was burned, the first step in Union General William T. Sherman's infamous "March to the Sea." Other commemorative plaques to the Battle of Ezra Church are in Mozley Park, northeast of the cemetery on Martin Luther King, Jr., Drive. Estimated Federal forces were 25,964 with losses of 607, compared with 12,723 Confederate forces, suffering losses of 4,632. Photograph by Allie Rivenbark.

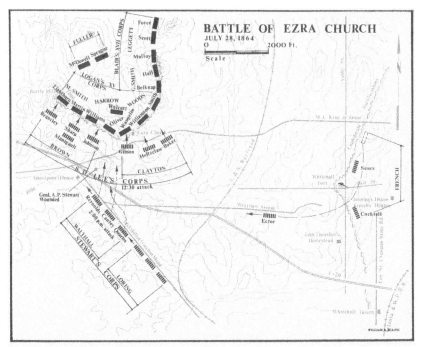

William Scaife's map of the Battle of Ezra Church. The Confederate front faced what is now Ralph David Abernathy Boulevard when the battle began. The zigzag line on the right of the map indicates the city fortification, as designed by L. P. Grant, and never breached. Map from Scaife's *The Campaign for Atlanta* scanned by Cash Barnes.

Edward Peter Clingman, 1842-1864, Section 70. The grave marker features modern carvings (1961) of a Confederate flag, pistol, and sword. The epitaph is badly worn. Clingman's grave was moved here in a ceremony 30 July 1961 conducted by the Sons of Confederate Veterans.

The McBurney Era, 1884-1930

Atlanta businessmen, led by Edgar Poe McBurney, a real estate developer, organized Westview in the summer of 1884, and the first burial took place that October. McBurney admired Woodlawn Cemetery (1863) in the Bronx in New York City, which had recently opened. Another model was Greenwood Cemetery in Cincinnati (1848).

McBurney, a native of New Jersey, joined his father in the real estate business in 1880. In addition to the cemetery, he established West View Floral Company in 1890. Greenhouses would continue to operate on the cemetery property until at least the 1950s.

A requirement of the cemetery's charter was that the city could use a portion for pauper burials. The "Potter's Field" at Oakland was exhausted. This practice—burials of both white and "colored" bodies, according to cemetery records—continued until approximately 1900. The area along the southeastern perimeter has now reverted to forest. None of the graves are marked.

An 1890 rulebook identifies Bellett Lawson as superintendent and landscape gardener. An early landscape gardener was Thomas W. Burford, who also managed the greenhouses. Burford had previously worked in England, and he is best remembered today for his discovery of the Burford holly, *Ilex cornuta burfordii*, during his tenure at Westview. The original tree formerly stood near the entrance gate. The Holly Society of America has installed a commemorative plaque there.

The rules stipulated that fences, hedges, curbing, and enclosures of all kinds were prohibited. This policy contrasts with the prevalent style of Oakland, where lots are typically set apart by curbing, and some fences still remain.

Westview became a prestigious place to be buried, particularly after the body of local hero Henry Grady (1850-1889), orator and champion of the New South, was translated from the Grant mausoleum in Oakland to an elegant mausoleum at Westview in 1892. While "old Atlanta" continued to use Oakland, Westview was catching on.

In 1908 Grady was joined at Westview by his former colleague from the Atlanta *Constitution*, Joel Chandler Harris, author of the Uncle Remus stories. His rusticated granite tombstone suggests more the Old South than the New.

McBurney managed Westview for nearly 50 years. During his tenure, automobiles, airplanes, a race riot, and a deadly flu epidemic all came to town. So did Coca-Cola.

When McBurney died in 1940, an editor of the *Journal* wrote, "Largely through his efforts, Westview, where he will be buried, was made into one of the most beautiful cemeteries in America."

Entrance Gate, Ralph David Abernathy Boulevard. The entrance gate, no longer in use, contains a bell tower; the bell formerly signaled funeral processions. The entrance gate was closed in 1975 when the new cemetery office was built; the gate itself was too narrow to accommodate cars comfortably. According to a 2008 study by the Cherokee Garden Club, the entrance gate was designed by George P. Humphries, but Jeff Clemmons has determined the architect to have been Walter T. Downing, and the date of construction, 1890. In 2014 Westview is considering using the gatehouse as a visitors' center. The structure, composed of "slick stone" quarried nearby, has 1940s-era extensions at each end, clad in the same Westview-quarried stone as the Abbey.

Tower Bell, Gatehouse. The bell is dated 1890. Photograph by Paul Hammock.

Helen Livingston Haskins, died 1884, Section 4. Mrs. Haskins's was the first burial at Westview Cemetery, just a few months after the cemetery was organized. Mrs. Haskins was the first wife of Charles R. Haskins, an attorney.

South-View Cemetery, 1886, Jonesboro Road. In 1886 a group of African-American businessmen founded a new cemetery on Jonesboro Road, from the beginning open to all races, but with a predominantly African-American clientele. In addition to general overcrowding at Oakland, the founders of South-View resented having to use a rear entrance to come and go, and that the so-called "Black Section" was low-lying and sometimes swampy. Among the founders was Albert Watts, the great-great uncle of the current president, Wini Hemphill. Notable burials at South-View include those of Alonzo Herndon, Martin Luther King, Sr., poet A. A. Whitman, and political potentate and patriarch John Wesley Dobbs. Photograph by Annie Kinnett Nichols.

Sisson children, 1887, Section 1. This chilling monument tolls the deaths of three children within eleven days. Infant mortality was common in the days before vaccines. Childhood diseases such as measles, mumps, and diphtheria were deadly. Vardy P. Sisson, their father, was a "newspaper man, printer, publisher, Confederate soldier, state legislator and city councilman," according to Franklin Garrett.

Receiving Vault, 1888, Section 4. A receiving vault was a necessary feature of cemeteries at the time Westview was founded. In case of inclement weather, frozen ground, or muddy conditions, bodies would be stored here awaiting burial. Construction of this vault, which had room for 36 caskets[7], began soon after the cemetery was founded. The inscription notes that the receiving vault was particularly useful during the flu epidemic of 1918, and that the vault was sealed in 1945, after the Abbey was built.

---

[7] Or 108. See Afterword.

Kate Lindsey Peters, 1847-1888, Section 1. The attractive but lonely grave marker features a copper quatrefoil embedded in a square stone frustum, with "DEAR MAMMA" carved into the top. Although Peters was a famous pioneer name, Kate has proven hard to track down.

Henry Woodfin Grady, 1850-1889, Section 50. Grady was editor of the *Constitution* and a tireless booster of Atlanta, the city he envisioned as the capitol of the New South. His vision of the post-Reconstruction South depended on Northern investment, cheap and willing Southern labor, and a progressive, pro-business attitude. Grady died after returning from a speaking trip; his funeral was held Christmas Day, 1889, at First Methodist Church. Grady's body was housed in the Grant mausoleum in Oakland Cemetery until this mausoleum in Westview was completed in 1892.

Henry Grady statue, 1891, Marietta Street. This monument by the noted sculptor Alexander Doyle has stood on Marietta Street near Five Points since 1891. Financed with public donations, the statue is near the former *Constitution* offices. During the race riot of 1906, two bodies of African Americans were dragged to the base of the statue, the mob's expression of scorn for Grady's New South optimism.

Grady Hospital, 1892, Coca-Cola Place. Grady is the largest hospital in the state of Georgia. The red brick building in front, known as Georgia Hall, dates from 1892. In old city vernacular, the hospital was called "The Gradys," since it had one side for whites and one side for blacks, separate but equal—or at least coincident—facilities. The civic esteem for Henry Grady, who was just 39 when he died, is evident: a high school and a hospital are named for him, as were the Henry Grady Hotel and a large housing project, Grady Homes.

Henry Holcombe Tucker, 1818-1889, Section 1. Tucker was president of Mercer University from 1866 to 1871, and chancellor of the University of Georgia from 1874 to 1878. He was the founding president of the Georgia Education Association in 1867, which favored "educating the blacks with equal privileges with the whites," yet stipulating they would be taught in separate schools. The city of Tucker is named for him.

Confederate Veterans' Monument, 1890, Trinity Section. The monument to Confederate veterans was built in 1890 by the Confederate Veterans' Association. The Georgia Confederate Soldiers' Home opened in July 1901 and burned 30 September. It was rebuilt the next year. In the 1950s, Franklin Garrett wrote, "Today no wearers of the gray occupy the Confederate Soldiers' Home. One by one, through the years, they were gathered to their fathers, and joined their old commanders, Lee, Jackson, Gordon, and Longstreet beyond the river." The last Civil War veteran residing in the Soldiers' Home died in 1924; the building was torn down in 1964. The decorations of the four faces of the pedestal include a snake swallowing its tail (representing eternity), a butterfly (representing rebirth or renewal), illustrations of the Biblical text "They shall beat their spears into ploughshares and their shields into pruning hooks. Nation will not take up sword against nation, nor will they study war anymore" (Micah 4:3) and the Lost Cause text "Of Liberty born of a Patriot's dream / Of a storm-cradled nation that fell" from the sentimental poem "Lines on the back of a Confederate Note" by Maj. Sidney Alroy Jonas (c. 1815-1915). A graveyard scene illustrates this. There are stacks of cannonballs, an Egyptianizing winged cannonball, and other items.

David Mayer, 1815-1890, and Elisa Weilmann Mayer, 1829-1902, Section 1. From its founding, Westview was open to Jews. The founding committee included prominent Jews Jacob Elsas and Jacob Haas. The various Jewish sections of Oakland exhibit different attitudes toward orthodoxy and assimilation; most Jewish burials at Westview tend towards the latter. The principal Jewish cemeteries in Atlanta today are at Greenwood (1909), Crest Lawn (1912), and Arlington (1922). David Mayer was born in Bavaria in 1815. He immigrated to the U. S. in 1839 and arrived in Atlanta in 1847. He worked for Joseph Haas, one of the first two Jews to settle in Atlanta in 1845. Mayer was a dry goods merchant; in 1859 he was worth $59,000 and owned six slaves. He also traded slaves, and was president of the Hebrew Benevolent Society, now known as The Temple. Mayer participated in the establishment of the Old Jewish Burial Ground in Oakland in 1860. He was a blockade runner in the Civil War and served on Governor Joseph Brown's staff. Known as the "father of public schools," he served on the board of education from its creation in 1869 until he died. He was also a worshipful master of the Fulton Masonic Lodge No. 216. Elisa Weilmann Mayer was a leading citizen and founder and president of the Grandmothers' Club, said to be one of the most exclusive organizations in the city in a *Constitution* article from 1898. A modern refurbishment of the weathered marble monument provides transcriptions of the weathered inscription, and translations of the Hebrew portions.

William Henry Peck, 1830-1892, Section 4. Peck was an editor, the author of 75 novels, and a poet, glorifying the Lost Cause. His epitaph reads, "Author, patriot, historian, of excellent wit and most ready pen, he nobly pleaded the cause of the South and endeared himself to a thousand readers. He left few enemies and many friends. His children can scarce support his loss, never replace his bright presence."

Daniel Norwood Speer, 1836-1893, Section 1. Cemetery scholar June Hadden Hobbs has observed that depictions of males in funerary art are usually portraits, while depictions of females are usually allegorical. Speer was a major in the Confederate army and a trustee of Georgia Tech. In 1889 the *Constitution* speculated that his net worth was approximately $750,000.

Lemuel Pratt Grant, 1817-1893, Section 1. During the Civil War, Grant, an engineer, was responsible for designing and implementing fortifications for the city to ward off Yankee attacks. In 1882, he donated 100 acres in Southeast Atlanta to the city to create a public park, known as Grant Park, the home of Zoo Atlanta and the Cyclorama[8]. The small obelisk on the left marks the grave of Grant's wife's first husband.

Grant mansion, 1856, Grant Park. The home of Lemuel P. Grant is one of only five remaining antebellum residences in Atlanta. The house, formerly two stories, served as a Confederate hospital during the Civil War, and was the birthplace of golfer Bobby Jones in 1902. It is now headquarters for the Atlanta Preservation Center, which sponsors an annual spring celebration of historic places and structures around the city called Phoenix Flies.

---

[8] In 2014 the city announced that the Cyclorama would move to the Atlanta History Center.

Auguste Paul Tripod, 1839-1894, Section 1. Born in Switzerland, Tripod served in the Confederate army and later was an art-supply dealer. Photograph by Traci Rylands.

William Jeremiah Garrett, 1825-1896, Section 4. A founder of Westview, Garrett had erected in his memory a striking monument, an angel atop a very tall pedestal up the hill from the Receiving Vault.

Thomas Warner Latham, 1843-1898, Section 1. Latham was a Confederate colonel, lawyer, and prominent businessman. His epitaph reads, "Blessed are the pure in heart for they shall see God." The back of the gravestone bears a symbol of the Knights Templar, a cross and crown surrounded by the motto "In Hoc Signes Vinces (in this sign you conquer)."

Latham House, c. 1890, Inman Park. Thomas Warner Latham's house at 804 Edgewood Avenue is one of the first built in Inman Park, now the Sugar Magnolia bed and breakfast. Before its restoration, the house was divided into 13 apartments. In Queen Anne style, it features a three-story turret, a grand staircase, six fireplaces, painted ceilings, and a crystal chandelier in its front hall. The Inman Park neighborhood, Atlanta's first suburb, is listed on the National Register of Historic Places.

George Washington Adair, 1823-1899, Section 1. George Washington Adair was the patriarch of a real estate, political, and social dynasty. In the Civil War he served as an aide to Gen. Nathan Bedford Forrest, and later he named one of his sons Forrest. The Adair Park neighborhood in Southwest Atlanta is named for the family. The grave marker, a sarcophagus-style monument surrounded by a dozen headstones for family members of identical design, is embowered by a magnolia tree.

Thomas Mason Brumby, 1855-1899, Section 6A. Brumby was a naval officer, credited with raising the flag over Manila in the Philippines, to signal the American victory in the Spanish-American War, 13 August 1898. He returned to Atlanta a hero, feted with a parade. Unfortunately, he died from typhoid fever three months afterwards, and this obelisk was erected in his honor when his remains were translated from Oakland Cemetery. Brumby's cousin Thomas Micajah Brumby was mayor of Marietta.

Water Tower, c. 1900, Trinity Section. Perhaps because of Atlanta's destructive fires—the city symbol is the Phoenix—water towers figure often in city constructions. The crenelated top of the water tower suggests a medieval castle. During his tenure at Westview, Asa Griggs Candler, Jr., had a trophy room, offices, and a cafeteria built around the polygonal building at the base. The water tower is no longer operational.

Laurent DeGive, 1828-1901, Section 1. DeGive, the Belgian consul in Atlanta, was the proprietor of an opera house (1871) downtown. A second opera house, DeGive's Grand Opera House, opened in 1893 at the corner of Peachtree and Forsyth Streets. It was later the Loewe's Grand Theater, the site of the premiere of the movie *Gone With the Wind* in 1939.

George Washington Collier, 1813-1903, Section 4. Collier was a large landowner; Collier Road, Collier Hills, and other sites attest to his renown and power in the city. Collier's antebellum house, much altered over the years, stands at 1649 Lady Marian Lane in the Sherwood Forest neighborhood in Ansley Park.

Virgil Orvin Hardon, 1851-1904, Section 1. Hardon, born in Massachusetts, studied medicine at Harvard and Bellevue Hospital Medical College. He was a medical doctor and professor at Atlanta College of Physicians and Surgeons, later known as Atlanta Medical College, and now Emory University School of Medicine. He was one of the first fifteen physicians in charge of Grady Memorial Hospital. His grave marker, densely inscribed front and back, gives his life story and résumé in thorough detail, including his having named his daughter for himself, Virgil Orvin Hardon. His specialty was gynaecicology, with its archaic spelling.

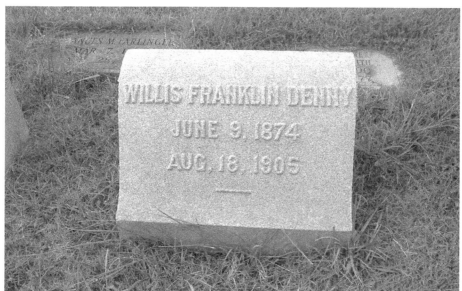

Willis Franklin Denny, 1874-1905, Section 1. Denny was born in Louisville, Georgia, and educated at Cornell University. He was an architect whose work can be seen today in Rhodes Hall and the Kreigshaber house, now the Wrecking Bar Brewpub. He also designed First, St. Mark's, and Inman Park Methodist churches. He died from pneumonia when he was only 31 years old.

Wrecking Bar, 1900, Moreland Drive. In the 1990s the Victor Kreigshaber house was an architectural antique store called the Wrecking Bar, selling artifacts salvaged from razed houses and other buildings. In 2011 it was renovated as an event space upstairs, a restaurant downstairs, and a brewery behind. North of the Wrecking Bar on Moreland are a pair of stone lions, which once marked the driveway to Denny's own home.

Lyman Hall, 1859-1905, Section 1. Hall was a West Point graduate, the first professor of mathematics and later the second president of Georgia Tech, serving from 1896 to 1905. Lyman Hall, formerly a chemistry laboratory, and now an administrative building on the Georgia Tech campus, is named for him. Photograph by Traci Rylands.

Evan Park Howell, 1839-1905, Section 5. The name Howell is memorialized in Howell Mill Road, an important west-side artery. The mill was operated by the Howell family on Peachtree Creek just northwest of the city. Evan Park Howell was a Confederate veteran, executive editor of the Atlanta *Constitution*, member of the state House of Representatives, and mayor from 1903 to 1905.

Livingston Mims, 1833-1906, Section 4. Livingston Mims was born in South Carolina and served in the Mississippi legislature before the Civil War. He was president of the Capitol City Club for more than 30 years. When he was mayor of Atlanta, 1901-3, he and his wife, Sue Hunter Mims, lived in a mansion at the corner of Peachtree Street and Ponce de Leon Avenue, the present site of the Georgian Terrace Hotel. During his term of office, he oversaw construction of the Whitehall Street viaduct and the Carnegie Library.

Capital City Club, 1910, Peachtree Street. The Capital City Club, founded in 1883, was and is a social club for powerful businessmen. The building at Peachtree Street and Harris Street (also known as John Portman Boulevard at Historic Harris Street) is sufficiently imposing: MEMBERS ONLY. The Capital City Club bought the Brookhaven Country Club in 1915.

Livingston Mims bust, Georgian Terrace. Today the Georgian Terrace features two restaurants, one called Livingston's and the other called Mims. Mims, putatively depicted in this bust now on display at Livingston's, was mayor of Atlanta. One of his accomplishments was to establish Mims Park, in the current Vine City neighborhood. It was the first Atlanta park to include a desegregated playground.

Ida E. Thompson, died 1906, Section 3. The race riot of 1906 occurred 22-26 September. It was provoked by inflammatory writings in both the *Journal* and the *Constitution*, claiming a rash of assaults on white women by black men. A governor's race was underway, and the candidates each had newspaper connections. Mrs. Robert C. Thompson was one of two white fatalities; she was "scared to death" by the rioting. The exact number of black fatalities is unknown, but at least 25 African Americans were killed.

Samuel Dexter Niles, 1829-1907, Section 1. Niles was born in New Hampshire. He was an educator and possibly a building contractor for Joel Hurt, who founded the Inman Park neighborhood in 1886. Photograph by Traci Rylands.

Niles House, 1888, Inman Park. Samuel Niles is rumored still to haunt the stairwell, where he fell to his death, in his former residence at 80 Spruce Street. The house has been an apartment house and a bordello, and the turret room was the scene of a murder.

Joel Chandler Harris, 1848-1908, Section 1. Harris was author of the Uncle Remus stories. After he published sketches in national magazines, his first book of Uncle Remus tales appeared in 1880. His popularity was exceeded only by Mark Twain's. President Theodore Roosevelt said, "Presidents may come and presidents may go, but Uncle Remus stays put!" The rusticated granite monument from the McNeel Marble Company features a portrait. Photograph by William Candler Bayne.

Wren's Nest, 1870, Ralph David Abernathy Boulevard. Harris bought this house in the West End neighborhood from George Muse in 1881. When the Harrises discovered a family of wrens had made their home in the front-porch mailbox, they named the house Wren's Nest.

Wren's Nest cenotaphs, 1908, Ralph David Abernathy Boulevard. After Harris died in 1908, his widow donated the Wren's Nest to the city. A year later a foundation was established to maintain and promote the house, the membership to consist of "one hundred white ladies." After the 1940s, the house museum went into a period of decline. The Disney movie *Song of the South*, innovative for its use of live actors together with animation, outraged African Americans for its demeaning depiction of blacks. A curious relic of the period is its "literary walk of fame," a sidewalk around the base of the house paved with cenotaphs of (white Southern) authors. In 2000, the Executive Directorship was entrusted to Lain Shakespeare, the energetic great-great-great grandson of the author. Along with careful restoration of the house, he started lively programs including storytelling, young writers' workshops, a website, and a blog.

Emma Mims Thompson, 1864-1908, Section 4. Emma Thompson, the daughter of Mayor Livingston Mims, was president of the Board of Lady Managers for the Cotton States Exposition, the world's fair held in Atlanta in 1895. Conferences held at the Women's Building gave rise to the Atlanta Woman's Club and local chapters of the National Council of Jewish Women and the National Association of Colored Women.

William Lycett, 1855-1909, Section 3. Lycett was an English-born artist, noted for his porcelain. His father, Edward Lycett, was a respected ceramicist, "the pioneer of china-painting in America," whose work included a White House commission for the Andrew Johnson administration. Lycett established a china-painting studio in Atlanta in 1893, and committed suicide in 1909.

Oliver Wiley Harbin, 1835-1910, Section 12. Harbin was the engineer of the locomotive the *William R. Smith* that pursued the *General* in the "Great Locomotive Chase" on 12 April 1862. The *General* had been stolen by the Andrews Raiders, a band of Union soldiers intent on destroying the rail line between Atlanta and Chattanooga.

Benjamin F. Abbott, 1839-1911, Section 1. Abbott, a lawyer, was one of the directors of the Cotton States Exposition. It is most remembered today for Booker T. Washington's "Atlanta Compromise" speech and the eventual establishment of Piedmont Park on the exhibition grounds. Abbott was married to the widow of banker Robert H. Richards (d. 1888), whose mausoleum is one of Oakland's most elaborate. The Richards-Abbott mansion was later the site of Macy's on Peachtree Street.

Thomas L. Langston, 1834-1911, Section 4. Langston was a grocer and the first president of Westview. He was also vice president of the West End and Atlanta Street Railroad, incorporated in 1883, which was extended to Westview by 1889. Photograph by Traci Rylands.

Harry C. Stockdell, 1836-1912, Section 12. Stockdell was the first president of the Capital City Club and the first potentate of Yaarab Shrine Temple. He was a city councilman and ran for mayor in 1904. There appears to be a misspelling on the plinth. Photograph by Traci Rylands.

Pellegrino Pellegrini, 1838-1913, Section 1. An Italian, Pellegrini manufactured terracotta. He was a member of the Yaarab Shrine Temple. Photograph by Traci Rylands.

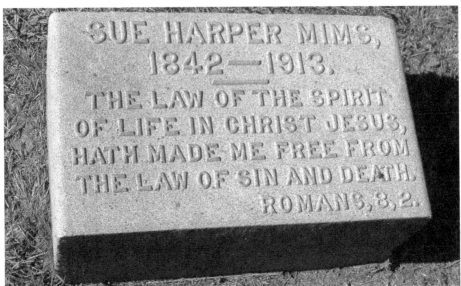

Sue Harper Mims, 1842-1913, Section 4. Sue Harper Mims was the second wife of Mayor Livingston Mims. While he was mayor, the Mimses hosted weekly lawn parties at their house at the corner of Peachtree Street and Ponce de Leon Avenue. Citizens could come and tell the mayor just what they thought. Mrs. Mims sold her jewelry to pay for the Sidney Lanier monument in Piedmont Park.

First Church of Christ, Scientist, 1914, Peachtree Street. Sue Harper Mims was active in the Christian Science church, having been instructed and healed by an envoy of Mary Baker Eddy in 1886. She was instrumental in the establishment of the First Church of Christ, Scientist, in Ansley Park at Peachtree and 15th. The building was designed by architects Arthur Neal Robinson and Edward Daugherty. The church claims to have been the first air-conditioned building in Atlanta, with large fans blowing air over blocks of ice in passages beneath the auditorium.

John Morton Smith, 1835-1913, Section 5. Smith was from 1869 a carriage maker who changed his profession when the automobile replaced the horse and buggy. The inexorable increase in cars started when William D. Alexander bought three steam-powered Locomobiles in 1901. In 1913, the carriage era ended when Smith burned "twenty-five phaetons, victorias and sulkies, which had a value of $30,000 in their day."

Jesse Parker Williams, 1842-1913, Section 5. One of the most famous monuments in Westview (see p. 55), this sculpture was carved by the renowned American sculptor Daniel Chester French, who famously carved the Abraham Lincoln statue in the Lincoln Memorial in Washington, DC. This is one of two French sculptures in Atlanta, the other of railroad magnate Samuel Spencer, formerly in front of Terminal Station, now on Peachtree Street near 15th Street. French's Kinsley monument at Woodlawn Cemetery in New York was the model for James S. Novelli's celebrated Thurman monument in Oakland Cemetery.

Emma E. Bell, 1843-1914, Section 5. Ms. Bell, a widow with two children, operated the Bell House, housing for bachelor men, from 1878 until her death. Residents were known as Bell House Boys, a sort of fraternity. The boarding house operated in various locations, and continued after her death, finally closing in 1957. The antique gas streetlight that formerly stood in front of the Bell House is now in storage at the Atlanta History Center.

Thomas Egleston, 1856-1914, Section 5. A founding member of the Capitol City Club, Thomas Egleston established a hospital for children that he named in memory of his mother, Henrietta Egleston. The elaborate funerary tableau features an epic Celtic cross with extensive carving and distinctive lettering, surrounded by a four-part exedra. This is the largest Tennessee pink marble cross in the US, executed by McNeel Marble Company.

Thomas Jefferson Hightower, 1829-1916, Section 4. Hightower was the original vice president of Westview Cemetery. Hightower Road in northwest Atlanta was his estate, later the site of the Atlanta Child's Home. The monument features Saint John the Evangelist.

Cleland Kinloch Nelson, 1852-1917, Section 5. Nelson served as the third Episcopal bishop of Georgia, 1892-1907, consecrated at St. Luke's, then as the first bishop of Atlanta when the diocese was divided in 1907. He admired philanthropist Thomas Egleston and wished to be buried near him. This Celtic cross is decidedly more modest than Egleston's.

George Muse, 1854-1917, Section 5. Muse was a clothier and civic leader. His farmhouse in the West End was rented to then purchased by Joel Chandler Harris, who enlarged it into the Wren's Nest. Muse was jury foreman in a trial following the 1906 race riot, and co-authored the official report on the riot, citing deaths at 12 black, two white. Research by Rebecca Burns and Cliff Kuhn indicates that the African-American death toll was at least double that.

Muse's, 1921, Peachtree Street. Muse's clothing store stood at Peachtree and Walton Street, the building designed by Philip Trammell Shutze. The store closed in 1992 and was later converted to Muse's Lofts, a block from Five Points and across the street from Woodruff Park. During the Civil War, this was the site of a Confederate arsenal.

Oscar Pappenheimer, 1861-1917, Section 5. Mr. and Mrs. Pappenheimer were both musicians, and their house on Ponce de Leon Avenue contained a large music room with a pipe organ, two grand pianos, and portraits of composers. The Pappenheimers hosted regular musical events from the 1890s to the 1920s, precursors to the Atlanta Symphony and Atlanta Opera. In the 1970s and 1980s the house served as an abortion clinic, notorious for its unsanitary conditions when it was closed in 1988. It was razed in 1999.

Benjamin Robert Padgett, Sr., 1850-1919, Section 9. Padgett was an early developer of the Virginia-Highland neighborhood, centered at the intersection of North Highland Avenue and Virginia Avenue, starting in 1893. The Highland Avenue Streetcar made commuting downtown convenient. Noted architect Leila Ross Wilburn (1885-1967) worked in Padgett's firm before opening her own office.

Alonzo Aron DeLoach, 1857-1921, Section 1. DeLoach was an inventor, as was his father, principally of devices useful in the milling industry. His inventions included the DeLoach Turbine Water Wheel and the DeLoach Friction Driven Saw Mill Engine, both widely used.

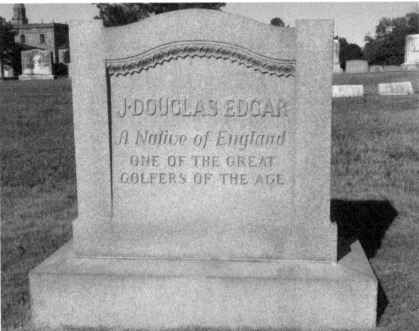

James Douglas Edgar, 1885-1921. Edgar was a golfer and mentor of Bobby Jones. He was born in Newcastle-upon-Tyne, England. Edgar won the Canadian Open in 1919—by 16 shots—and 1920. His mysterious death was rumored to have stemmed from a love affair with a married woman. He bled to death on West Peachtree Street from a leg injury. No arrest was ever made. Photograph by Traci Rylands.

Wilbur Fisk Glenn, 1839-1922, Section 1. Glenn was an Emory alumnus, a Methodist minister for 50 years. He was pastor of First Methodist Church 1884-6.

Glenn Memorial United Methodist Church, 1930, Emory. The church on the campus of Emory University is named in honor of Wilbur Fisk Glenn, the building designed by Atlanta favorite Philip Trammell Shutze. The principal donors were Glenn's children Thomas Kearny Glenn, a banker and president of Atlantic Steel, and Flora Glenn Candler, wife of Coca-Cola president Charles Howard Candler (all are buried at Westview). The pipe organ was formerly in the Asa Griggs Candler, Sr., mansion on Ponce de Leon Avenue. In the building behind Glenn Memorial Church is Shutze's "Little Chapel," based on a design by Sir Christopher Wren, often used for weddings for Emory students.

Hyatt Meshach Patterson, 1851-1923, Section 5. H. M. Patterson & Son has been a leading mortuary in Atlanta since 1883. Patterson's handling of the funeral of Georgia Governor and former Confederate Vice President Alexander Stephens in 1883 was lauded in the *Constitution*, "It was universally pronounced the most successfully managed large funeral ever held in Atlanta." Photograph by Robert Parks.

H. M. Patterson & Son Spring Hill Mortuary, 1928, Spring Street. The Spring Hill Chapel on Spring Street was designed by Philip Trammell Shutze. Frank Bowen, who would later buy Westview, worked on the construction of the mortuary, and became involved in other aspects of the mortuary business with Patterson as a result. The chapel has been the setting of many famous funerals, including that of Margaret Mitchell in 1949.

Frank Mason Robinson, 1845-1923, Section 5. Robinson coined the name Coca-Cola for Dr. John Pemberton's medicinal concoction of coca leaves, cola nuts, and other secret ingredients. Robinson's handwritten Coca-Cola script was adopted for the company logo. Photograph by Robert Parks.

Coca-Cola sign, Five Points. The corporate symbol is one of the most recognized trademarks in the world. In Eudora Welty's 1943 story "The Wide Net," Hazel's not-very-bright cousin "Edna Earle could sit and ponder all day on how the little tail of the 'C' got through the 'L' in a Coca-Cola sign." Edna Earle Ponder would later star in Welty's comic novel, *The Ponder Heart* (1953).

Frank Henry Gaines, 1852-1923, Section 10. Gaines was the founding president in 1889 of Decatur Female Seminary, now Agnes Scott College. He wrote a history of the college, published in 1922. Photograph by Traci Rylands.

Luther Zeigler Rosser, 1859-1923, Section 5. The Leo Frank murder case is one of the most notorious in Georgia history. The victim, Mary Phagan, worked in a pencil factory where Frank, a northern Jew, was an executive. Frank was convicted and sentenced to die by hanging. Two appeals failed. Governor John Slaton, on his last day in office, commuted Frank's sentence to life in prison. A mob stormed the prison in Milledgeville where Frank was held, kidnapped him, drove him to Marietta, and lynched him. Rosser was lead defense attorney for Frank, and later a judge.

Ossian Daniel Gorman, 1841-1924, Section 3. Gorman was a poet. According to his obituary, he "contributed poetry to the *Constitution* and leading magazines for 30 years. He was founder and editor of the Talbotton, Georgia *Standard*." He also served as superintendent of public schools in Talbotton. Photograph by Traci Rylands.

Cora Best Taylor Williams, 1860-1924, Section 5. Mrs. Taylor, the widow of Jesse Parker Williams, succeeded her husband as president of the Florida, Georgia, and Alabama Railroad. Whereas the principal statue on the monument, a signed sculpture by the celebrated Daniel Chester French, is allegorical (could that be Audrey Munson?), the monument also contains presumed bas-relief portraits of the Williamses (see p. 45). Cora Best Taylor Williams's will established the Jesse Parker Williams Foundation to promote the health of women and children.

Maud Maria Barker Cobb, 1870-1925, Section 1. Cobb was assistant state librarian for the state of Georgia, 1904-7, then state librarian from 1907 until her death. The state archives were formerly housed in Rhodes Hall and then in a building, now abandoned, across Memorial Drive from the Capitol. Cobb is also memorialized by a cenotaph at Oconee Hill Cemetery in Athens. Photograph by Traci Rylands.

John Temple Graves, 1856-1925, Section 5. Graves was born at Willington Church, Abbeville County, South Carolina. He was a newspaper editor, orator, and writer (*The Fighting South*). He was a grand-nephew of South Carolina politician and U. S. Vice President John Caldwell Calhoun, and a candidate himself for Vice President in 1908, for the People's Party. Temple composed "the immortal toast," whatever that is, recited annually by members of the Kappa Alpha Order, and was a defender of lynching. Photograph by Robert Parks.

William Thomas Gentry, 1854-1925, Section 1. Gentry, a Virginia native, came to Atlanta in 1884 to manage the Atlanta Telephone Exchange. He rose through the ranks to become president of Southern Bell. His house in East Lake was intended to lure others to the area near East Lake Country Club, "a playground for the wealthy elite." The Capital City Club purchased Brookhaven Country Club during his presidency. The golf associations are curious, given that Gentry had only one arm as a result of a childhood accident. Photograph by Traci Rylands.

Southern Bell Building, 1929, Peachtree Center Avenue. The Art-Deco pile has some interesting ornaments, including statues of a stylized telephone line repairman and an operator above the main entrance. The original design called for 25 stories; the 1929 structure was in fact only six stories tall. Subsequent additions increased its size to the current 14 stories. Photograph by William Candler Bayne.

Henry Elliott Harman, 1866-1926, Section 5. A native of Lexington, South Carolina, Harman was a poet and an editor of trade journals. His books included *Gates of Twilight* (1910), *Dreams of Yesterday* (1911), *A Bar of Song* (1913), and *Idle Dreams of an Idle Day* (1917). He died in Miami from a self-inflicted gunshot. He told his family he was going to the garden to shoot a stray cat. The only witness was his grandson.

George E. Murphy, 1850-1926, Section 4. Murphy was the architect and builder of the Candler Building. Its V shape, providing cross-ventilation for separate office towers, is repeated in the Hurt Building and others downtown. Murphy also built Candler's Inman Park home, Callan Castle, and Inman Park Methodist Church. Photograph by Traci Rylands.

Frank Lebby Stanton, 1857-1927, Section 4. A native South Carolinian, Stanton wrote a newspaper column and sentimental poetry, published in the Atlanta *Constitution*. Some of his poems were set to music, the most popular of these being "Mighty Lak' a Rose" and "Just A-Wearyin' for You." An oft-recited poem in its day, "This World," is quoted on his tombstone. He was appointed the first poet laureate of Georgia in 1925. Frank L. Stanton Elementary School, just north of Westview, and the surrounding Mozley Park, were reassigned from whites to African Americans in 1954 after a five-year struggle.

James Edward Dickey, 1864-1928, Section 4. Dickey was a Methodist bishop and served as the last (twelfth) president of Emory College and the first president of Emory University, holding the position from 1902 to 1915. He was pastor of both Grace and First Methodist churches.

Frances Newman, 1883-1928, Section 4. Newman published two novels, *The Hard-Boiled Virgin* (1926) and *Dead Lovers are Faithful Lovers* (1928). She was a critic for the Atlanta *Journal* and *Constitution*, and also a translator and literary scholar. Her first novel concerns a southern woman torn between her traditional Atlanta mores and those of the Jazz Age, and choosing the latter. There is no dialog and no paragraphing. It was banned in Boston.

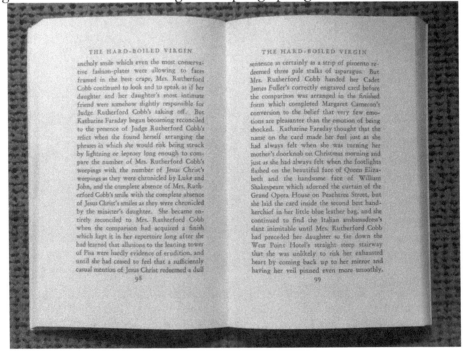

Amos Giles Rhodes, 1850-1928, Section 1. Rhodes was the founder of Rhodes Furniture and partner of J. J. Haverty. The Rhodes-Haverty alliance lasted from 1889 to 1906, and was revived in the 1920s when they joined forces to construct the Rhodes-Haverty Building on Peachtree Street.

Rhodes Hall, 1904, Peachtree Street. Amos Rhodes's mansion on Peachtree Street, Rhodes Hall, designed by Willis Franklin Denny, formerly served as the Georgia State Archives, and is now an event space. The design is evocative of Rhineland castles. Constructed of Stone Mountain granite, it features a crenellated tower, a round stairwell with stained-glass windows depicting the history of the Confederacy, a large wraparound porch, and a porte-cochère. Rhodes Hall, nicknamed "the castle on Peachtree," is also headquarters for the Georgia Trust for Historical Preservation.

Asa Griggs Candler, Sr., 1851-1929, Section 4. Coca-Cola was a game changer for the city of Atlanta. The drink began humbly as a medicinal cure-all, cleverly mixed with sparkling water, purchased by an ambitious salesman. Asa Griggs Candler, Sr., created the Coca-Cola Company and became Atlanta's richest man. In the course of time, Candler became mayor, one brother became a bishop in the Methodist Church, and another was named a justice on the Georgia Supreme Court. Candler served one term as mayor of Atlanta, 1917-1919. Photograph by Allie Rivenbark.

Callan Castle, 1902, Elizabeth Street. Candler's Inman Park house (1902) at the corner of Elizabeth Street and Euclid Avenue is called "Callan Castle" after the ancestral home in Ireland. The Candler coat of arms is depicted in stained glass on either side of the front door. The builder was George E. Murphy.

Candler Building, 1906, Peachtree Street. The Candler Building, situated "Where Peachtree Meets Sweet Auburn," and viewed here from the south, was the tallest building in Atlanta from 1906 until 1929. When it was built, it was the northernmost commercial building in the city, considered "far out" and remote from the business district.

Candler Building entrance, 1906, Peachtree Street. The Atlanta skyline changed when the Candler Building appeared on Peachtree Street, the tallest structure in town. It is clad in Georgia marbleand richly ornamented. A frieze features medallion portraits of Asa Candler's heroes, including Shakespeare, Beethoven, Michelangelo, Benjamin Franklin, Cyrus McCormick, and others. The family coat of arms is carved over the entrance, and is depicted on door plates throughout.

Candler mansion, 1916, Ponce de Leon Avenue. Candler's "lemon pie" house in Druid Hills was the costliest home in Atlanta when it was built for $210,000 in 1916. It is now the John Chrysostom Melkite Church. The house featured a stained-glass-covered sunken atrium, now the nave of the church.

Josiah Percival Stevens, 1852-1929, Section 5. Stevens was president of an engraving company. He was also an inventor, and received patents for a new design for a safety razor, a sash holder, an engraving machine, and other metal devices. The monument was executed by the McNeel Marble Company of Marietta. Photograph by Traci Rylands.

Sallie Tallulah Harman Cox, 1855-1929, Section 5. The wife of attorney and state legislator Albert Hill Cox, Cox was a founder of the Atlanta Woman's Club. She was also a member of the Daughters of the American Revolution. Photograph by Traci Rylands.

Atlanta Woman's Club, Wimbish House, Peachtree Street, 1898. The Atlanta Woman's Club was founded in 1895. The Wimbish House was designed by Walter T. Downing and purchased by the AWC in 1920. Anne B. Jones's *A Light on Peachtree: A History of the Atlanta Woman's Club* (2012) recounts the accomplishments of the AWC from its founding to the present day.

Trees Atlanta champion Gingko tree. Photograph by Cindy Julian.

Adair Interregnum 1930-4

Edgar Poe McBurney retired from management of Westview in 1930. He sold the property to members of the Adair family, who held it for three and a half years. The principals were Jack and Forrest Adair, Jr., grandsons of Col. George Washington Adair (1823-1899). The progenitor came to Atlanta in 1854. His various enterprises included newspapers, railroads, and auctioneering, but his main occupation was real estate. Before the Civil War he opposed secession, but he became an ardent Confederate supporter after Georgia seceded. He served under Gen. Nathan Bedford Forrest.

An 1877 history of Atlanta states that real estate "was a comparatively new business, which, in a few years, assumed immense proportions. In 1865 George W. Adair opened a bureau for the sale and exchange of real estate property. In the six years following, prices ran up to enormous and most unhealthy figures—millions of dollars changed hands."

After the war, he was president of the Georgia Western Railway, a director of the Piedmont Exposition, and an early member of the Capitol City Club. He was also a Fulton County commissioner, and wrote a real estate column for the *Constitution*, "Atlanta Dirt."

The Adair family has been active in the real estate business since the end of the Civil War, and remain so today. Adairs and others were early investors in the Druid Hills neighborhood, along with Hurts, Candlers, and Arkwrights. They are numerous at Westview. Forrest Adair (1865-1936) was active in the Yaarab Shrine Temple and an advocate for the establishment of the Scottish Rite Hospital. He was campaign manager for Asa Griggs Candler's mayoral race in 1916. Jack Adair (1913-1974), a driving force in the establishment of the Atlanta Civic Center, was president of the Capital City Club, Chamber of Commerce, Atlanta Real Estate Board, and National Alumni Association for Georgia Tech.

Perry Adair was a golfer, one of the "Dixie Whiz Kids" who toured with Elaine Rosenthal, Alexa Stirling, and Bobby Jones to raise money for the Red Cross in 1919.

Ernest Hartsock, 1903-1930, Section 9. Hartsock was a poet, editor of the influential poetry magazine *An Atlanta Argosy* at Oglethorpe University, and founder of Bozart Press, established in 1927 to promote Southern literature. This title was chosen clearly in response to H. L. Mencken's 1917 damning essay "Sahara of the Bozart," lamenting the sorry state of Southern literature at the time. Hartsock died when he was only 27. The bronze marker bears Hartsock's poem "Second Coming."

Bust of Ernest Hartsock, Oglethorpe University, Peachtree Road. The statue was executed in 1932 by sculptor Fritz Paul Zimmer.

Daniel McKenzie Bain, 1847-1931, Section 4. Bain was a Scot, a Confederate private (he enlisted when only 15), and a founder of the Burns Club. He served as president of the Young Men's Library Association, a forerunner of the Atlanta Public Library. He assisted the ailing Henry Grady off the train the day before he died, and participated in the last visit of Jefferson Davis to Atlanta, escorting him to the podium for his speech to the crowd. He killed Gus Williams but was acquitted of murder charges in 1909.

Burns Cottage, 1911, Grant Park. The Burns Club was organized in 1896 to celebrate the life and poetry of Scotland's favorite bard, Robert Burns (1759-1796). Activities include an annual Burns dinner on his birthday, 25 January, presumably with haggis, neaps and tatties, and considerable whiskey. The Burns Cottage, a replica of the poet's house in Scotland, was designed by architect Thomas Morgan.

Beaumont Davison, 1864-1932, Section 1. Davison, born in England, was a founder of Davison's department store. Davison's, variously Davison & Douglas, Davison-Paxon-Stokes, and Davison-Paxon, opened in 1891, and was the chief rival to Rich's downtown. The store was sold to Macy's in 1925, but retained the Davison's name until 1986. Xernona Clayton, a television personality and King family friend, bought mourning clothes there for Coretta Scott King in 1968. Photograph by Traci Rylands.

Davison-Paxon, 1927, Peachtree Street. The Macy's building, designed by Atlanta favorite Philip Trammell Shutze, occupies most of the city block on Peachtree Street between Ellis Street and Andrew Young International Boulevard. After Macy's closed in 2003, the building served as a telecommunications meeting point for a number of years before being converted in 2009 to an event space, called 200 Peachtree.

Harriett Harwell Wilson High, 1862-1932, Section 4. After her husband, merchant Joseph Madison High, died, Harriett High donated her house on Peachtree Street and 15th to the city as an art gallery. The collection was principally that of J. J. Haverty. The house served as the city's premiere museum, the High Museum, until the Richard Meier-designed building replaced it in 1983.

High Museum, Peachtree Street. In 2002 the museum was greatly enlarged, the further buildings designed by Renzo Piano. The grounds feature works by Roy Liechtenstein and Auguste Rodin, the latter statue a bronze entitled "The Shade," a gift from the government of France to the city as a memorial to the 106 arts patrons from Atlanta who died in a Paris plane crash in 1962, at the time the worst-ever aviation disaster.

Matsotaro Yoshinuma, 1891-1932, Section 10. Yoshinuma owned an Asian restaurant. The Japanese lettering is very rare in Westview. Photograph by Annie Kinnett Nichols.

Annie Adair Foster, 1869-1934, Section 1. A member of the famous Adair family, Mrs. Foster was a noted bridge player, according to Franklin Garrett. The bridge craze of the 1920s and '30s is described in Gary Pomerantz's book *The Devil's Tickets*. Foster filed for a U. S. patent for printed bridge scorecards in 1914. She was the daughter of patriarch George Washington Adair, and a member of the Daughters of the American Revolution.

The Candler Era, 1934-51

Asa Griggs Candler, Jr., the second son of the founder of the Coca-Cola Company, was probably Atlanta's most colorful millionaire—only Ted Turner would rival him. He was born in Atlanta and attended Emory. He bought Westview from the Adairs in 1934 for $600,000.

Earlier he had built a speedway south of the city, and raced cars there. When airplanes arrived, he converted the raceway to an airport, Candler Field. It eventually became Atlanta Municipal Airport, then Hartsfield Atlanta International Airport, and then in 2004 Hartsfield-Jackson International Airport, in memory of Atlanta mayors William B. Hartsfield and Maynard Jackson.

Candler's house, Briarcliff, sported a 1700-square-foot music room, called De Ovies Hall in honor of Raimundo de Ovies, dean of St. Philip's Cathedral from 1928 to 1947. It held the largest pipe organ in a private American residence at the time, with 4 manuals and 88 ranks of pipes. That organ is now at Wesleyan College in Macon. A second organ, the "solarium organ" from Briarcliff, would come to Westview in the 1940s, to serve in the Abbey chapel.

Once while on vacation Candler bought a circus, and had all the animals shipped by train to Decatur. The menagerie did not please his Druid Hills neighbors, who complained of the smell and the noise, escapees, and even attacks. Eventually he donated the animals, which included elephants named Coca, Cola, Pause, and Refresh, to Zoo Atlanta. Later he took up big game hunting, and his trips to Alaska, Montana, and Africa yielded a different kind of animal collection—trophies, for which he built a display room at Westview.

The trophy room, part of a complex at the base of the water tower that also included offices, a cafeteria, greenhouses, and a power plant, was demolished in the 1970s.

Candler's most ambitious project was the Abbey, a spectacular community mausoleum, deep within the Westview property. The Abbey was built by the "dean of mausoleum engineers," Cecil Eldridge Bryan, and designed by architect Charles Lee Jay. They had collaborated on Sunnyside Mausoleum (1921), now Forest Lawn-Long Beach, California, and on Mountain View Mausoleum (1935), Altadena, California. By the time Abbey construction began in 1943, Bryan had completed more than 60 community mausoleums around the country, employing a drainage and ventilation system he had patented in 1913. Westview Abbey was the "greatest and most important structure of his long and illustrious career." When he died in 1951, Bryan was credited with having built 80 mausoleums.

At the same time, Candler developed new areas of the cemetery in the memorial park style, that is, with no upright monuments, but instead with bronze grave markers flush with the ground. This modern style was first established at Forest Lawn Memorial Park in Glendale, California, in 1917. Its founder, Hubert Eaton, argued that mismatched, decrepit tombstones were gloomy reminders of death, whereas sweeping lawns with well-chosen statuary were representative of Life and Beauty. Eaton's "Builder's Creed" asserts that traditional cemeteries are "unsightly stoneyards, full of inartistic symbols and depressing customs." His scheme was "as unlike other cemeteries as sunshine is unlike darkness, as

Eternal Life is unlike Death," consisting of "a great park, devoid of mis-shapen monuments and other customary signs of earthly Death. . . ."

Cecil Bryan shared these ideas, writing, "We hope to see the day when it will be a national movement when the beautiful landscape will no longer be disfigured by the present unkempt and unwholesome graveyard, but have in its place beautiful and everlasting temples surrounded by well kept lawns and parks."

In addition to the landscape design, Forest Lawn also provided a full array of services, including mortuary, crematory, reception areas, catering, and so forth, all available for purchase "pre-need." Candler intended the same—there had been greenhouses at Westview from its earliest times—but the funeral home and crematory were never realized.

From at least 1945 the management of the cemetery was mainly the work of Florence Stephenson Candler, the second wife, and before that secretary, of Asa Candler, Jr. His first wife had died in 1927, and he remarried within a year. Evidence of Florence Candler's efforts include the Florence Candler Chapel in the Abbey, and more importantly, her having hired young Martha Powers, who lived in the neighborhood, to work at Westview in 1945. Powers has been employed there ever since. She remembers Mrs. Candler as a good businesswoman and organizer, and recalls the day Mrs. Candler told her she would retire.

Asa Candler, Jr.'s interest in the cemetery had waned by 1950. The Abbey was incomplete, and 250 families of people buried at Westview had sued him for "desecration" because of his landscaping efforts. He replied that he endeavored to bring Westview out of the horse-and-buggy days by adopting the modern memorial park style. He cited Lincoln Memorial Cemetery in Washington, with its flush metal grave markers. "If the Lord lets me live long enough and the people of Atlanta will cooperate, Westview will be the most beautiful place in the world." By early 1951, he agreed to sell the cemetery for $2 million to professional cemetery operators from Washington and the Midwest, led by L. O. Minear, who would take on the $350,000 potential liability owed to litigants and hold the cemetery for a year until local ownership could be assembled.

This description is from Candler's 1951 essay, "Self-Surrender":

> I have given much attention in recent years to the building of Westview Cemetery. People normally think of a cemetery with sadness and sorrow—a place of death. It is my purpose to make Westview a place where men's hearts and minds are lifted to God and immortality, to Life. A good sermon lifts the heart to God, unites the mind and the will with the purpose and gladness of God. It is my plan to make of Westview, and especially of its abbey, a whole series of sermons in stone and marble. . . . Within the chapel, as you see Christ's life in colored glass, you will hear the organ softly playing. That organ was in my own home for many, many years.

The remarkable panoramic photograph on the following page from 1939 depicts the Westview staff. On the far left is Candler's 1939 Cadillac limousine. His chauffeur stands beside it. Next is Candler in a white suit, carrying a cane. In the center is the uniformed grounds staff, with power mowers, tractor, truck, and Woody. Further right stand the laborers, in overalls, with mule cart, push mowers, and rakes. (Photograph from the collection of Westview Cemetery, Inc. Photograph by Christian Moreno.)

George Valentine Gress, 1846-1934, Section 6A. Gress donated the Cyclorama to the city. A cylindrical oil painting viewed from the interior, "The Battle of Atlanta" was commissioned by John A. Logan, a Union army general during the Atlanta Campaign. In 1884, he ran for vice president, and commissioned this painting for his campaign. Logan lost his race, and died soon afterwards. The painting languished for several years before coming into the hands of Gress, who was also an early benefactor of the zoo. This is the tallest obelisk at Westview, just under 30 feet.

Cyclorama, 1921, Grant Park. In the 1930s, a diorama was constructed, with figurines by Wilbur G. Kurtz occupying the space between the painting and spectators. In 2014 it was announced that the Cyclorama would move to the Atlanta History Center.

George Edward King, 1851-1934, Section 5. King founded a successful hardware company, with multiple stores around the city. He was the half-brother of Clyde King, president of the King Plow Company. The monument features a colonnade pergola surrounding a veiled urn.

King-Keith House, 1890, Inman Park. George King, the hardware magnate, built an impressive house in Inman Park, at 889 Edgewood Avenue. The King-Keith house was considered a neighborhood "Grand Dame" in the 1890s. By the 1960s the neighborhood was a wreck. Today the house and many others have been restored, and Inman Park is thriving. The King-Keith house was operated as a bed and breakfast inn until 2014.

John Sanford Cohen, 1870-1935, Section 4. Cohen was born in Augusta to a Jewish father and an Episcopalian mother; he was reared an Episcopalian. He was president of the Capitol City Club, 1918-9. He was appointed U. S. senator 25 April 1932 by Governor Richard B. Russell, Jr., to fill the vacancy caused by the death of William J. Harris. He served until January 11, 1933, when his successor—the same Richard B. Russell, Jr., who would serve in the Senate for nearly 40 years—was sworn in.

Alfredo Barili, 1854-1935, Section 7. Barili was a musician, born in Florence, Italy. His father sang the first Rigoletto in America, and his aunt was the great soprano Adelina Patti. Barili was a composer and music teacher, operating the Barili Music School with various members of his family. He was killed by a city bus near his house at the corner of Myrtle Street and Ponce de Leon Avenue.

Clark Howell, 1863-1936, Section 5. Clark Howell was the son of Mayor Evan Park Howell. He was editor of the Atlanta *Constitution*, becoming managing editor when Henry Grady died. He served in the Georgia House and Senate, and was a candidate for governor at the time of the 1906 race riot. Both the *Constitution* and the *Journal* (opposing fellow journalist M. Hoke Smith) fired up a mob by printing provocative stories about male African Americans' assaults on white women. Howell later won the Pulitzer Prize for journalism for exposing corruption in the office of Mayor Isaac Ragsdale. Georgia Tech and the University of Georgia both have buildings named for him.

Mary Millen Wadley Raoul, 1848-1936, Section 1. Raoul was a prominent clubwoman, belonging to the Daughters of the American Revolution, the United Daughters of the Confederacy, and the Colonial Dames, among others. She was also an active suffragette.

Rufus Thomas Dorsey, 1873-1937, Section 5. Dorsey holds the distinction of having scored the first touchdowns in college football games, both in Alabama and in Georgia. He later served as a physician and surgeon, and his brother, Hugh Mason Dorsey, was Georgia's governor.

Isaac Newton Ragsdale, 1859-1937, Section 5. Ragsdale served as mayor of Atlanta from 1927 until 1931, having formerly been mayor of Oakland City. During his time in office, the Atlanta graft ring corruption scandal arose. Twenty-six city emloyees were indicted by a grand jury and 15 were convicted or pled guilty. The *Constitution* was awarded the 1931 Pulitzer Prize for its coverage.

Robert Cotten Alston, 1873-1938, Section 4. Alston was founder of the Alston and Bird legal firm, the largest in Atlanta. Alston hailed from a distinguished Southern family, prominent in the Lowcountry of South Carolina as well as in Georgia. He belonged to the Capitol City, University, and Piedmont Driving Clubs. He is honored with an endowed chair at the University of Georgia Law School. This large cross, made of pink Tennessee marble, was manufactured by the McNeel Marble Company of Marietta.

St. Luke's, 1909, Peachtree Street. The Alston family's support of St. Luke's Episcopal Church is very evident—the church boasts the Alston Memorial Organ, one of the finest in the city, and the Alston Memorial Bell Tower (2000), with 10 change-ringing bells and a columbarium. The church was founded in 1864 in the immediate aftermath of the destruction of Atlanta.

Jack Johnson Spalding, 1856-1938, Section 5. Spalding was the founder with Alexander Campbell King (1856-1926, buried at Oakland) of the law firm King and Spalding. He was praised by Henry Grady in the *Constitution* and was general counsel for the Cotton States and International Exposition in 1895. He was president of the Atlanta Historical Society at the time of his death.

Cathedral of Christ the King, 1936, Peachtree Road. J. J. Spalding was a devout Roman Catholic, committed to the establishment of the diocese (now archdiocese) of Atlanta and the construction of the Cathedral of Christ the King. He was a Knight of St. Gregory, a Knight of Malta, and a recipient of the Laetare Medal from the University of Notre Dame. Because of the churches nearby the area is sometimes called "Jesus Junction."

Henry Morrell Atkinson, 1862-1939, Section A1. Atkinson was a banker before becoming majority stockholder of Georgia Electric Light Company in 1892, now Georgia Power. By 1894 a reporter for the *Constitution* wrote, "There is not a better lighted city in America than Atlanta." He was chairman of the board of Georgia Power from 1926 to 1939. His epitaph reads, "He put to work for Georgia the mountain streams that for centuries had run to waste."

John Rucker Dickey, 1857-1939, Section 5. Dickey founded the Atlanta Stove Works. He was the great uncle of the poet and novelist James Dickey (1923-97). Dickey served as Grand Commander of the Knights Templar.

Beath-Dickey-Griggs House, c. 1890, Inman Park. The mansion at 866 Euclid Avenue was the home of John Rucker Dickey. It was originally built for John M. Beath, president of Atlanta Ice and Coal, as a wedding gift for his wife. In 1969, Robert Griggs bought the house, then with 34 tenants, for $22,000, and undertook the first restoration in the then-decrepit neighborhood. The streetlamp and ornament atop the "belvedere" turret are original, as are gas lamps and fireplace tiles depicting native Georgia wildlife.

James Joseph Haverty, 1858-1939, Section 31. Haverty with Amos Giles Rhodes formed the Rhodes-Haverty Furniture Company in 1889. He was a serious art collector whose donations formed the nucleus of the High Museum. Francis Palmer Smith, designer of the Rhodes-Haverty building, also designed the Haverty mausoleum, constructed by McNeel Marble Company. The gothic mausoleum features a stained-glass window and two exedra.

Basilica of the Sacred Heart of Jesus, 1897, Peachtree Center Avenue. By 1893, Haverty was influential in the establishment of a "north side" Catholic parish, the time when the northern fringe of the city was still south of North Avenue. Designed by Walter T. Downing, the church and its handsome spires were the tallest structures in the city until they were eclipsed by the Candler Building in 1906. Sacred Heart Church was promoted to a basilica in 2010.

Rhodes-Haverty Building, 1929, Peachtree Street. The Rhodes-Haverty building (center), now a Marriott hotel, was designed by Francis Palmer Smith. It formerly housed Brooks Brothers on the ground floor. The "Golden Fleece" logo is visible, and "Brooks Brothers" is carved over the door on Williams Street. Haverty collaborated with his former partner to build the Rhodes-Haverty building directly across Peachtree from the Candler Building (left) in 1929. It held the record as the tallest building in Atlanta until 1954.

Candler and Rhodes-Haverty Buildings, Peachtree Street. Amos Giles Rhodes and J. J. Haverty were partners in the furniture business from 1889 to 1908, and joined forces again to construct the office building 20 years later. Now both the Candler and Rhodes-Haverty buildings are dwarfed by their neighbors, the Equitable Building (right, 1968, 453 feet) and the Georgia-Pacific Building (left, 1982, 697 feet). The tallest building in Atlanta is now (2014) the Bank of America Tower at Peachtree Street and North Avenue. Built in 1992, it stands 1040 feet. This photograph was taken at the Sundial, the revolving restaurant on the top floor of the Westin Peachtree Plaza hotel, built in 1976, 723 feet.

Harold D. Hirsch, 1881-1939, Section 4. Hirsch was the general counsel for Coca-Cola. He was a director of the Trust Company of Georgia, the Municipal Opera Association, the Atlanta Art Association, and the Stone Mountain Memorial Association. He was president of The Temple, 1930-4. In 1935, he arranged for the secret formula for Coca-Cola to be shared with Rabbi Tobias Geffen of Congregation Shearith Israel to determine the drink's kosher status. Geffen required that one ingredient (glycerine) in the recipe be changed.

James Lee Key, 1867-1939, Section 16. Key was mayor for four terms, the first two 1919-23 and the second two 1931-7. He opposed Prohibition and blue law bans on baseball and movies, and arranged for Works Progress Adminstration-funded repairs to the Memorial Auditorium and the Cyclorama. Photograph by Robert Parks.

Frederic John Paxon, 1866-1939, Section 5. Paxon was born in Philadelphia and came to Atlanta in 1887. The Davison-Paxon-Stokes department store was the chief rival to Rich's after 1891. Davison's was bought by Macy's in 1925, but the competition was intense until Rich's was bought by Federated Department Stores, effectively merging the two stores, in 1990. Paxon was chairman of the board of the store from 1927 until he died. He was president of the Chamber of Commerce, served on the boards of directors of myriad businesses, and belonged to various social, athletic, and fraternal organizations.

Paul Donehoo, 1885-1940, Section 11. Donehoo, blind from the age of five and half, was city coroner for 32 years. He was graduated from Mercer University, and attended Klindworth Conservatory of Music and Atlanta Law School. After he died, his wife ran for the job of coroner, a late entrant into the race against 47 opponents, and won.

Edgar Poe McBurney, 1862-1940, McBurney lot. McBurney organized Westview Cemetery in 1884. He admired Woodlawn Cemetery in the Bronx in New York City, which had recently opened (1861), and regarded it as a model for Westview. He also operated a nursery on the cemetery property; greenhouses stood here from 1890 until the 1970s. His is the second tallest obelisk in the cemetery, a little over 29 feet. The reader can check the estimate using the yardstick in the photograph. The obelisk is situated in a triangle between the graves of Henry Grady (visible on the far left) and Asa Candler, befitting the cemetery manager of 46 years.

Arthur Montgomery, 1854-1940, Section 4. Montgomery was a founder of the Coca-Cola Bottling Company, which he ran from 1903 until he died.

Dixie Coca-Cola, 1891, Edgewood Ave. This 1891 building at the corner of Edgewood Avenue and Courtland Avenue housed the Dixie Coca-Cola bottling plant. It is now the Baptist Student Center of Georgia State University. In the photograph the building undergoes repairs after a car crashed into it in 2013. The building is listed on the National Register of Historic Places.

Guido Negri, 1886-1942, Section 26. Negri owned Herren's restaurant from 1939, when he bought it from the prizefighter Red Herren. Herren's was one of the first restaurants in Atlanta to integrate, voluntarily, in 1962. Negri's son Ed (buried at Arlington Cemetery in Sandy Springs) took over management of the restaurant after World War II and operated it until 1987. Photograph by Traci Rylands.

Herren's, Luckie Street. Herren's was converted to a theater in 1995 by donors Bill and Peg Balzer, the first theater in the United States to be LEED certified (Leadership in Energy and Environmental Design) by the Green Building Council. It is the home of the Theatrical Outfit, called the Balzer Theater at Herren's. The troupe, overseen by artistic director Tom Key since 1995, has championed plays based on literature of the South. Photograph by William Candler Bayne.

Abbey exterior, 1943-5. The Abbey architecture is Spanish Renaissance Plateresque, in the style of a silversmith. The building is constructed of reinforced concrete, a material the builder regarded as indestructible. The exterior is faced with stone quarried on the Westview property. The same facing is evident in the 1940s extensions to the gatehouse.

Abbey interior, 1943. The Abbey (begun 1943) is one of the largest public mausoleums in the country, the work of architect Clarence Lee Jay and the foremost mausoleum builder of the 20th century, Cecil Eldridge Bryan. Bryan worked for a year for Frank Lloyd Wright and then for Ralph Modjeski, who was an early proponent of reinforced concrete. He built an estimated 80 mausoleums between 1912 and 1951. The Abbey interior is finished in 35 different kinds of marble. Many of the stained-glass windows, excluding the chapel, were executed at the Monastery of the Holy Comforter, Conyers, Georgia.

Chapel, 1943-5, Abbey. The Abbey's Florence Candler Chapel, named for Asa Candler, Jr.'s second wife, features stained-glass windows and a fan-vaulted ceiling. The chapel was used for the wedding of the daughter of a California artisan, Mr. Laylacker, who lived in an apartment onsite during construction. The chapel was also used for a wedding scene in *Fast and Furious 7*, which was being filmed in Atlanta when its star, Paul Walker, died in 2013.

Chapel reredos, 1943-5, Abbey. The carved reredos in the chapel, with painted panels and an Ascension theme, is likely the work of R. Brownell McGrew, who executed similar artwork for Sunnyside Mausoleum, now Forest Lawn-Long Beach. The organ loft surrounds the reredos. The chapel vestibule or narthex has four paintings depicting Christian parables, by Benjamin Mako, who also designed the stained glass, 27 scenes from the life of Christ. The chapel windows were made by the Los Angeles Art Glass Company.

Mortuary, 1943-5. During construction of the Abbey, legislature was passed that forbade funeral homes from operating within a cemetery; thus, the one-stop shopping ideal could not be realized. Its planned elevator, leading to the embalming chambers on the third floor, was never installed. The large reception or family room, equipped with a fireplace and a sweeping view of the terraces and former lake, is now unused.

Loggia, 1943, Abbey. The Abbey decorations include heraldic motifs, shields, and escutcheons, and the carvings on the loggia, the east end of the building, are elaborate. They include the seals of the State of Georgia and of the City of Atlanta (see page vi).

Cartouche, 1943, Abbey. This medallion on the exterior wall of the Abbey, just past the porte-cochère, commemorates the building and Westview's then-owner, Asa Griggs Candler, Jr. It combines the initials of West View Abbey with those of Asa Candler and the date, 1943, emblazoned.

Aerial photographs of Westview c. 1943 and c. 1945. The Abbey would go in the clearing near the top in the older photograph, just right of center. In the lower photograph, the Abbey tower hasn't yet been completed. Collection of Westview Cemetery, Inc. Photographs by Christian Moreno.

The Abbey, c. 1945. No Abbey tower, still. This photograph was used on a postcard. Lake Palmyra would be drained in the 1970s. That name is now attributed to a different lake further west in the cemetery. Collection of Westview Cemetery, Inc. Photograph by Christian Moreno.

Aerial photograph of Westview, c. 1945. The Abbey tower is visible. Buildings at the base of the water tower in the lower right included greenhouses and a trophy room. While the Abbey was under construction a large portion of the cemetery was "opened up" in the memorial park style—lawns of graves with flat bronze markers. A new entrance was created on the north, just left of center top in the photograph, an entrance to the Memorial Park. Collection of Westview Cemetery, Inc. Photograph by Christian Moreno.

Trophy Room, c. 1945. Displaying the big-game-hunting treasures of Asa Griggs Candler, Jr., "two of everything," but in this photograph there is no African elephant, which didn't arrive until 1947. Its weight compromised the structural integrity of the building until its eight-foot tusks were removed. The West View Electric Company operated at the western end of the property. The greenhouses were the largest in the South. Collection of Westview Cemetery, Inc. Photograph by Christian Moreno.

Henry Charles Heinz, 1879-1943, Section 5. Heinz was a banker, Kiwanis president, and the second husband of Asa Griggs Candler, Sr.'s daughter Lucy. In 1943, Heinz, interrupting a prowler, was shot to death in the library of their home, Rainbow Terrace. A neighbor and a policeman were also wounded in the confusion, and the murder mystery dragged on until a burglar confessed to the crime a year and a half later. Some visitors claim to have witnessed ghostly phenomena at the house. Bill Owens was Lucy's first husband.

Rainbow Terrace, 1922, Ponce de Leon Avenue. The former residence of Lucy and Henry Heinz, Rainbow Terrace was designed by G. Lloyd Preacher. After Heinz's murder, the house was abandoned, and fell derelict for decades, until being converted to condominiums. It was divided into three units, and other buildings were constructed around it to complete the complex. Photograph by William Candler Bayne.

Edward Emmett Dougherty, 1876-1943, Section 1. Dougherty was graduated from the University of Georgia and studied architecture at the Ecole des Beaux Arts in Paris. He was architect of the Venable mansion, Stonehenge, on Ponce de Leon Avenue, now St. John's Lutheran Church. He also designed the Imperial Hotel on Peachtree Street, Druid Hills Baptist Church at the corner of North Highland Avenue and Ponce De Leon Avenue, and the Veterans Memorial Building in Nashville.

Charles Davis Tillman, 1861-1943, Section 4. Charlie Tillman was a musician, known for his popular gospel tune, "Old Time Religion," featured in the Academy Award-winning film *Sergeant York.* His footstone features musical notation, a line from his hit "Life is Like a Mountain Railroad."

Ernest Woodruff, 1863-1944, Section A1. Wealthy from Atlanta and Edgewood Street Railroad and the Trust Company of Georgia, Ernest Woodruff bought the bulk of Coca-Cola shares from the children of Asa Griggs Candler, Sr., just after Candler retired from the company in 1919 and divided most of his stock among his children.

"Small" Woodruff House, 1890, Inman Park. Designed by architect Gottfried Normann, Ernest Woodruff lived at this house at 882 Euclid Avenue for about 10 years after he moved from Columbus to run the Edgewood Street Railroad. Two other Inman Park houses have Woodruff connections, the brick mansion to which Ernest moved after this one, on Edgewood Avenue, and a Robert Woodruff house, now the Inman Park Bed and Breakfast on Waverly Way.

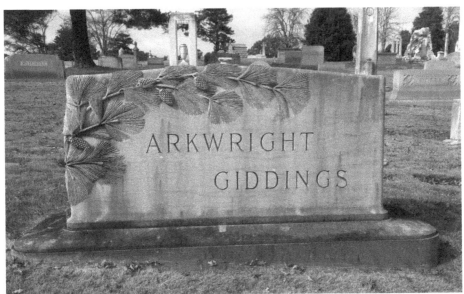

Preston Stanley Arkwright and Dorothy Colquitt Arkwright, both 1871-1946, Section 5. Preston Arkwright was president of Georgia Railway and Electric Company, now Georgia Power, and owner of the Atlanta Crackers baseball team. With George and Forrest Adair and Asa Candler, he was an early investor in Druid Hills. Dorothy Arkwright was the daughter of former governor and U. S. Senator Alfred Holt Colquitt (1824-94). Photograph by Traci Rylands.

Pinebloom, Druid Hills. The Arkwrights' home, on South Ponce de Leon Avenue, was a social center for decades, accommodating weddings, Easter egg hunts, fraternity parties, and so on. It is now part of Jackson Hill Baptist Church. Photograph by William Candler Bayne.

Joseph Regenstein, 1874-1946, Section 10. Regenstein operated a clothing store downtown, in a building built for the Peters Land Company.

Regenstein's department store, Peachtree Street. Originally the Peters Land Company, this building is rendered in Art Deco style, designed by Francis Palmer Smith of the architectural firm of Pringle and Smith. The building now houses Hooter's restaurant.

Zella E. Richardson, 1868-1946, Section 5. Married to Alonzo Richardson, Zella Richardson was president of the Atlanta Woman's Club 1923-4. She petitioned the city for representation on a traffic committee, saying "strictly manmade" traffic laws neglected the needs of women. Photograph by Robert Parks.

Nan Bagby Stephens, died 1946, Section 4. Stephens was a playwright, composer, and librettist. She wrote a Broadway play, *Roseanne*, and the libretto for an opera by composer Amy Beach, *Cabildo*, about the imprisonment of pirate Jean Lafitte in New Orleans in 1812. She also composed settings for the poems of Frank Lebby Stanley.

William Fleming Winecoff and Grace S. Winecoff, 1870-1946, Section 35. The tallest hotel in the Southeast at the time, the Winecoff Hotel advertised itself as a fireproof building, and indeed it was. Unfortunately, the *contents* of the hotel, the bedding, carpet, curtains—and most tragically, the guests—were decidedly not. On 7 December 1946, fire broke out on the third floor of the hotel, full of visitors for Christmas shopping, or attending a YMCA convention. Smoke and flames rose through the stairwells and elevator shaft, trapping people on the upper floors. Fire ladders couldn't reach that high. Some people were able to fashion ropes from bed sheets, or to jump onto nearby buildings or into firemen's nets, but 119 people died. This tragedy remains the worst hotel disaster in US history. The Winecoffs lived on the tenth floor of the hotel and perished in the fire.

Winecoff Hotel, 1946, Peachtree Street. This vintage photograph shows the Winecoff Hotel fire, 7 December 1946, in which 119 people died. It was the worst hotel disaster in US history. Other hotels proclaimed their "absolutely fireproof" qualities, including the Hermitage in Nashville and the Monteleone in New Orleans. As a result of the calamity, national fire safety codes were strengthened. Photograph printed with permission of Kenan Research Center at the Atlanta History Center.

Ellis Hotel, 1913, Peachtree Street. Today the hotel operates as the Ellis, a boutique hotel at the corner of Peachtree and Ellis Streets, across from the Ritz Carlton. A historical marker describing the Winecoff fire formerly faced Peachtree Street, but is now more discreetly positioned on the south side of the building. Some ghost-hunters claim to have heard screams or other kinds of frenzied activity in the upper floors.

Margaret Alston Refoule, 1916-1947, Section 4. A member of the prominent Alston family, Margaret Alston married a French artist. He taught art at Oglethorpe University and at the High Museum. In 1947, Mrs. Refoule's body was found in Peachtree Creek with her shoes tied together. The ensuing investigation revealed that art students had posed nude for each other and that Refoule may have engaged in affairs with his students. Mr. Refoule was suspected of the murder, which was never solved.

Walter Henry Rich, 1880-1947, Section 5. Rich was president of Rich's department store. He was the nephew of Morris Rich, who founded the dry goods store in 1867. For nearly 100 years, Rich's was a retail institution, providing notable coconut cakes, a Pink Pig railway for children, a Christmas tree-lighting event, and other amenities. Rich's famously accepted scrip, paid to teachers and other city workers, during the Great Depression.

Rich's, 1924, Broad Street. The clock on the chamfered corner has been an Atlanta landmark since Rich's flagship store, designed by the firm of Hentz, Reid and Adler, opened at the corner of Broad and Alabama in 1924. Dr. Martin Luther King, Jr., was arrested for attempting to be served in Rich's Magnolia Room diner in 1960. The building now serves as office space for federal government workers, part of the Sam Nunn Federal Complex.

Hugh Manson Dorsey, 1871-1948, Section 5. Dorsey was the prosecuting attorney in the Leo Frank case, and later served two terms as governor of Georgia, from 1917 to 1921. He was the author of *The Negro in Georgia.*

Samuel Green, 1890-1949, Section 10. Green was an obstetrician and Georgia Grand Dragon of the Knights of the Ku Klux Klan in the 1940s. He was elected Imperial Wizard of the organization in 1949 but died two weeks later.

Samuel Candler Dobbs, 1868-1950, Section B. Dobbs was a first cousin once removed of Asa Candler, Sr. He served as president of the Coca-Cola Company from 1919 to 1922, after Candler retired and notably when the Candler heirs sold their inherited stock to Ernest Woodruff. Dobbs was president of the Associated Advertising Clubs of America, later the American Advertising Federation. In 1939 he donated $1 million to Emory University. Emory University grants Dobbs professorships to honor young faculty members.

Lucile King Thomas Smith, 1882-1951, Section 5. Smith was president of the Atlanta Woman's Club from 1918 to 1921, during which time AWC purchased the Wimbish House on Peachtree Street and expanded its footprint and operations. The daughter of hardware mogul George Edward King, she was married first to Irving Thomas (1867-1922) and after he died to Claude Smith (1873-1959). The Lucile King Thomas Auditorium, built in 1922 at the AWC, is named in her honor. It is now the nightclub Opera.

The Bowen Era, since 1952

Charles Bowen, Sr., recalls when his father, Frank Coll Bowen, and five others bought the cemetery from Asa Griggs Candler, Jr., at the Briarcliff Hotel in 1952. The sale included all the enterprises, the greenhouses, the power plant, and the trophy room. For about a year prior the property had been held by a consortium of cemetery professionals led by L. O. Minear of Washington, DC.

The other investors included R. B. Nelson, an officer of the Family Fund Life Insurance Company, and as a silent partner Fred Patterson, the president of H. M. Patterson and Son Mortuary. Bowen, with a building background, had known Patterson from having worked on the Spring Hill chapel, and operated the Wilbert Burial Vault Company[9]. The "silence" of the Patterson involvement was due to Candler's dislike of Patterson. It's likely that Candler's thwarted desire to establish a funeral home and crematory at Westview in the 1940s contributed to their mutual disdain.

When the purchase was announced, Bowen and Nelson took out a newspaper ad, vowing to assure families that they would respect their wishes regarding the physical landscape.

Westview Cemetery, Inc., has operated since then as a nonprofit organization.

The trophy room, constructed from materials salvaged from Candler's Briarcliff laundry, in ill repair, and a complex that included a cafeteria and the reputedly largest greenhouse in the Southeast, have been demolished. The trophies were donated to Fernbank Science Center, but have since been lost. Some were destroyed because of insect infestation. The power plant was decommissioned.

In the more than 60 years that the Bowen family has operated the cemetery, a number of large Italian marble sculptures have been added to the memorial park sections of the cemetery, depicting the Good Shepherd, Eternal Life, and so on. These were executed by the McNeel Marble Company of Marietta. Another large installation is a bas relief representation of Da Vinci's Last Supper, of poured concrete, by the German-born artist Fritz Paul Zimmer (c. 1875-1975), who was an art professor at Oglethorpe University. This was originally a fountain, and was created onsite. The molds for the sculpture are part of the Westview archives.

The chapel pipe organ, formerly Candler's "solarium organ" at Briarcliff, having fallen into disrepair, was traded for a Hammond electronic organ to the Rev. Roy O. McClain (c. 1916-1985). McClain, who served as pastor of Atlanta's First Baptist Church from 1953 to 1970, was an organ hobbyist. He also bought a Wurlitzer theater organ from the Howard Theater, later renamed the Paramount, when the theater was demolished in 1959, and installed it in his house in Sherwood Forest. After he retired to Orangeburg, South Carolina, McClain donated the Aeolian organ to Charleston Southern University, but it has

---

[9] Burial vaults, or concrete grave liners, prevent graves from sinking as coffins decay. These have been required in most cemeteries since the 1930s. Before burial vaults were popularized, families would mound dirt over graves to account for the sinking. Removal of these mounds was what pissed off the lot owners. The Bowen family still head the Wilbert Funeral Services Company, as it is now known, in Georgia.

since been replaced by a Möller instrument. The whereabouts of the Aeolian instrument are unknown.

The whites-only policy of the cemetery changed with the passage of the Civil Rights Act of 1964, but it was possibly a decade or more until the first African-American burials took place. The surrounding neighborhood had undergone a "white flight" transformaion starting in the 1940s. For several years a portion of Hunter Street, Westview's northern border, was renamed Mozley Drive to distinguish white and black sections. By the end of the decade, Frank L. Stanton Elementary School and Mozley Park had been designated as black. Hunter Street is now Martin Luther King, Jr. Drive.

A new office building was built in 1975, designed by Henry Howard Smith, the son of Francis Palmer Smith. Prior to this addition, the cemetery offices had been located in the gatehouse or in the mortuary building.

In 1984, in response to increasing popularity of cremation, Westview built a modern columbarium in the Abbey courtyard.

The Westview archives include cemetery records dating to the founding of the cemetery in 1884, maps, mausoleum blueprints, and photographs.

The cemetery maintains its dignified appearance and mien, and is an active enterprise, conducting multiple burial and inurnments each week.

In 2014 Westview participated in the Phoenix Flies program of the Atlanta Preservation Center. More than 200 visitors took guided tours of the grounds and Abbey mausoleum. Encouraged by this public interest, Westview hopes to undertake preservation projects, in particular to use the 1884 gatehouse as a visitor's center and exhibition space, to make known the cultural and historical significance of the cemetery.

Last Supper bas relief by Fritz Paul Zimmer.

Charles Augustus Sheldon, Jr., 1884-1952, Section 19. Sheldon was a Doctor of Music. He played the organ at the Temple, the principal Reform synagogue on Peachtree Street, and served as official organist for the City of Atlanta. In the latter role, he was called upon to respond to a false report that President Woodrow Wilson had died, issued while the Vice President, Thomas R. Marshall, was speaking in Memorial Auditorium, 23 November 1919. He played the then-current expression of public grief, namely the hymn "Nearer, My God, To Thee," as reportedly played by the band as the *Titanic* sank in 1912.

Marion Luther Brittain, 1865-1953, Section 5. Brittain was president of Georgia Tech from 1922 to 1944. Emory University's Marion Luther Brittain Award is its highest student honor. Photograph by Traci Rylands.

Asa Griggs Candler, Jr., 1880-1953, Section 2. Candler's spending habits were catholic and lavish. He liked fast cars, and built a speedway south of downtown. He decided he liked planes even better, and converted his racetrack to an airport, Candler Field, the forerunner of Hartsfield-Jackson. He collected exotic animals, and bought a menagerie from a failing circus when he was on a European vacation. He owned Westview Cemetery from 1933 to 1951. Photograph by Allie Rivenbark.

Briarcliff Hotel, 1924, Ponce de Leon Avenue. Candler spent his final years living in the penthouse of the Briarcliff Hotel, which he built at the corner of Ponce de Leon Avenue and North Highland Avenue. The architect was G. Lloyd Preacher. The hotel has variously been known as the 750, the Briarcliff Hotel, and 191. That Al Capone stayed here is a debunked myth. Today (2014), under renovation, the building, known as the Briarcliff Summit, provides senior housing.

Briarcliff, 1922, Briarcliff Road. Candler's mansion gave its name to Briarcliff Road, the northern extension of Moreland Avenue. The house featured a music room in which was installed the largest pipe organ in a private house in America at the time. The organ was donated to Wesleyan College in Macon in honor of his wife, where it is now known as the Goodwyn-Candler-Panoz Memorial Organ, one of the largest pipe organs in the Southeast, with four manuals, six divisions, and 89 ranks totaling 4,932 pipes. The grounds included a swimming pool, a zoo, and an amusement park. Eventually Candler donated his menagerie, including elephants named Coca, Cola, Pause, and Refresh, to Zoo Atlanta. The house was sold to Emory University, and served for several years as a mental rehabilitation hospital and alcohol treatment center. The estate, with the ruined mansion, now forms the Briarcliff Campus of Emory.

James Charles Jacob Bagby, Sr., 1899-1954, Section 35. "Sarge" Bagby was a Major League baseball pitcher. In 1920 he went 31-12 and led the Cleveland Indians to their first World Series victory. In the Series, he hit the first home run by a pitcher. Ty Cobb called him the smartest pitcher he ever faced. His son Jim Bagby, Jr. (1916-88) was also a Major League pitcher, and is also buried at Westview. Photograph by Traci Rylands.

John R. Gunn, 1887-1956, Section 39. Gunn was a minister and syndicated columnist, the author of twelve inspirational books. Photograph by Traci Rylands.

Madge Alford Bigham, 1874-1957, Section 16. Bigham was the author of *Aunt Fanny's Kitchen* and *Sonny Elephant*. Graduating college in 1890, she started and ran the Atlanta Free Kindergarten until the Depression. She was a noted author of children's books, and her home was Hammonds House in the West End, now a museum of African-American art. Photograph by Robert Parks.

Augusta M. "Gussie" Brenner, 1866-1957, Section 4. Brenner was principal of the Fair Street School. In 1920 she lobbied for a facility to provide for disabled children before the Atlanta Public School Teachers' Association. Photograph by Traci Rylands.

Charles Howard Candler, 1878-1957, Section 4. Howard Candler succeeded his father, Asa Griggs Candler, Sr., as president of the Coca-Cola Company. He was chairman of the board of trustees of Emory University. Candler's wife, Flora Glenn Candler, was the daughter of Wilbur Fisk Glenn, the Methodist minister for whom Glenn Memorial United Methodist Church at Emory is named.

Callanwolde, 1920, Briarcliff Road. The Asa Griggs Candler, Sr., homes in Inman Park and on Ponce de Leon Avenue appear almost modest compared to the estates built by his sons. Charles Howard Candler's "Callanwolde," a monster Tudor revival mansion on Briarcliff Road, included greenhouses, tennis courts, stables, and a built-in player Aeolian pipe organ. It is now an arts center.

Medora Field Perkerson, 1892-1960, Section B. Mrs. Perkerson was an author, best known for her book *White Columns of Georgia.* She was an advice columnist, "Marie Rose," in the *Atlanta Journal-Constitution Magazine,* edited for decades by her husband, Angus Millard Perkerson. She was a friend and mentor to Margaret Mitchell.

Carling Dinkler, c. 1900-1961, Section 31. The Dinkler Plaza Hotel, called variously the Hotel Ansley and the Dinkler Ansley, was a prestigious hotel in the Fairlie-Poplar district. Dinkler owned hotels in various cities, including the Tutwiler in Birmingham and the Andrew Jackson in Nashville. In 1961, Dinkler jumped from the 12th floor of the hotel, a shocking suicide. In 1964, the Dinkler Plaza was the site of Atlanta's first integrated formal dinner, held in honor of Dr. Martin Luther King, Jr.'s receipt of the Nobel Peace Prize.

Roby Robinson, Jr., 1908-1962, and Louise Phinizy Calhoun Robinson, 1916-1962, Section 5. Roby Robinson was a member of the Capital City Club, an executive with the *Constitution*, and director of an investment firm started by his father, Robinson-Humphrey. Louise Calhoun Robinson founded the Peachtree Garden Club. They died in the 1962 Paris plane crash that killed more than 100 Atlanta arts patrons. Photograph by Traci Rylands.

Tryggvesen, 1923, Buckhead. The Robinsons' house was a pink palace, formerly 100 landscaped acres facing West Paces Ferry Road. It was built for Mrs. Robinson's father, Andrew Calhoun. The architect was Philip Trammell Shutze. Enrico Caruso never sang here, contrary to a persistent legend, having died in 1921. The former driveway to the estate is now Pinestream Road. Photograph by William Candler Bayne.

Sarah Lowe Latimer Clay Benson, died 1962, Section 5. Sally Benson was first married to Alexander Stephens Clay III, a lawyer who died in a plane crash in 1945. After his death she married Dr. Marion Benson, chief of staff and head of obstetrics at St. Joseph's Hospital. She died in the Orly plane crash 3 June 1962. Photograph by Traci Rylands.

Rodin Sculpture, Memorial Arts Building, 1968, Woodruff Arts Center. This sculpture, "L'Ombra" or "The Shade," memorializes the 106 Atlantans, many of them art patrons, who died in the Paris plane crash, 3 June 1962.

Lucy Beall Candler Owens Heinz Leide, 1883-1962, Section 5. The only daughter of Asa Griggs Candler, Sr., Lucy first married William Owens in 1903. They lived on South Ponce de Leon Avenue in a house called The Goose, later part of the Paideia School. It burned in 2009. Owens died in 1914, and Candler next married banker Henry Heinz. They lived at Rainbow Terrace on Ponce. There in 1943, Heinz was murdered during a burglary. After the tragic event, the house stood abandoned for decades; eventually it was converted into condominiums. In 1946 she was married to cellist and conductor Enrico Leide.

Henrietta Celeste Stanley Dull, 1863-1964, Section 14. Mrs. Dull managed the Soldiers' Recreation House, serving soldiers stationed in Atlanta during World War I. Her articles on cooking were a popular feature of the Atlanta *Journal* for 20 years. Her cookbook, *Southern Cooking* (1928), is still in print. Mrs. Dull lived to be 100.

Hiram Wesley Evans, 1881-1966, Section B. Evans was Imperial Wizard of the Ku Klux Klan, 1922-39. He joined the Dallas, Texas, Klan in 1920, and within two years became the national leader. In 1923 he led a Klan gathering of over 200,000, the largest ever, in Kokomo, Indiana.

Wilbur George Kurtz, 1882-1967, Terrace E. Kurtz was an artist and historian. He founded the Pen and Brush Club of Atlanta, and was a founding member of the Atlanta Historical Society, the forerunner of the Atlanta History Center, and of the Civil War Round Table. His watercolor paintings and sketches depict Atlanta at various stages of its history. He also built the Cyclorama diorama and supervised the 1934-6 restoration of the painting. On the recommendation of Margaret Mitchell he worked as a consultant for the film version of *Gone With the Wind*. Photograph by Traci Rylands.

Tullie Vilenah Smith, 1885-1967, Abbey. Smith was the last family member to live in the Tullie Smith House, built by her great-great grandfather, Robert Smith. She was renowned for her six feet, one inch stature, her sense of humor, and her tenacity not to sell the landmark house and property. Photograph by Christian Moreno.

Tullie Smith House, 1837, Atlanta History Center. The Smith farm in north Decatur (c.1840) on North Druid Hills Road was moved to the Atlanta History Center in 1969. The complex includes a barn, a corncrib, and other outbuildings. Photograph by William Candler Bayne.

Ivan Earnest Allen, Sr., 1876-1968, Section 5. An Atlanta saying is that "there's more power in the Chamber of Commerce than in City Hall." A stationer, Ivan Allen was elected president of the Chamber of Commerce during World War I. His wealth and influence increased as the Ivan Allen Company became one of the largest office-supply companies in the nation. The history of the Allen family, together with that of African-American patriarch John Wesley Dobbs, is told in Gary Pomerantz's book *Where Peachtree Meets Sweet Auburn.*

Ralph Emerson McGill, 1898-1969, Section 48. The tradition of talented and powerful editors at the Atlanta *Journal* and *Constitution* is noteworthy. McGill, born at Soddy-Daisy, Tennessee, near Chattanooga, came to Atlanta in 1929 and rose through the ranks to become editor of the *Constitution.* His columns were nationally syndicated, and he was known particularly for his anti-segregationist writings. He won the Pulitzer Prize for editorial writing in 1959 and the Presidential Medal of Freedom in 1964.

Deryl E. Horsey Sharp, 1882-1969, Section B. Sharp was the wife of Norman Sharp. According to Rosalynn and Jimmy Carter, she urged the mayor in 1925 for the city to purchase a landing field. He appointed her to the City Landing Field Committee, and she was later elected First Vice President of the Atlanta Chapter of the National Aeronautical Association. She was president of the Atlanta Woman's Club 1924-6.

Enrico Leide, 1887-1970, Section 60. Leide, born in Italy, was a musician. He played cello and conducted both classical and popular music. He was the conductor of the Atlanta Symphony Orchestra from 1920 to 1930, and was the third husband of Lucy Beall Candler, the only daughter of Asa Candler, Sr.

Dorothy Rogers Tilly, 1883-1970, Trinity Section. Tilly was active in Methodist women's organizations and a Civil Rights activist. She founded the Fellowship of the Concerned, to end discrimination in the courts, police brutality, and voter registration problems. In 1947, she was appointed to President Truman's Committee on Civil Rights and co-authored its report. She was a member of the American Palestine Committee to Israel, and lobbied in Washington for the Farmer's Union. Photograph by Traci Rylands.

Ezzell Neal Pattillo, 1896-1971, Section B. Pattillo was the wife of Howard Pattillo. She was a longtime member and president of the Atlanta Woman's Club, 1940-3.

William Berry Hartsfield, 1890-1971, Section 13. Hartsfield was mayor for more than 20 years. He was a champion of air transportation, and proclaimed Atlanta to be the "City Too Busy to Hate" during the early days of the Civil Rights movement. His name is remembered now for Hartsfield-Jackson International Airport, the busiest in the world.

Willie B., 1961-2000, Zoo Atlanta. A monument to Hartsfield was a beloved gorilla at Zoo Atlanta, Willie B. He was the dominant male for 30 years, and his death made front-page news in 2000. This statue, which contains the gorilla's cremated remains, is a popular feature at the zoo. Photograph by William Candler Bayne.

Francis Palmer Smith, 1880-1971, Section 13. Architect of various churches, residences, and educational and commercial buildings, Smith led the architecture school at Georgia Tech from 1909 to 1922. The firm of Pringle and Smith designed Regenstein's, the William-Oliver Building, and others, as well as the standard Coca-Cola bottling plant, replicated across the country. Robert Craig, professor emeritus of Architectural History at Georgia Tech, calls him the most accomplished Atlanta architect of his generation. Photograph by Traci Rylands.

Cathedral of St. Philip, 1962, Peachtree Road. St. Philip's is the oldest Episcopal church in Atlanta, founded in 1846. The church formerly stood downtown across from the state capitol, and moved to Buckhead in 1933. The building, designed by Francis Palmer Smith, commands the intersection of Peachtree Road and Andrews Drive, "Jesus Junction."

Geoffry Lloyd Preacher, 1882-1972, Section 31. Preacher was an architect, most notably of Atlanta City Hall, shown below; the Henry Grady Hotel, demolished in 1974; the Briarcliff Hotel; Rainbow Terrace; and the Medical Arts Building at the corner of Peachtree Street and Ralph McGill and Ivan Allen, Jr., Boulevards, endangered as of 2014.

City Hall, Mitchell Street, 1930. Gothic Deco. Photograph by William Candler Bayne.

Hal Fitzgerald Hentz, 1883-1972, Section 5. The architectural pantheon in Atlanta, both residential and commercial, features Neel Reid and Philip Trammell Shutze, neither of whom is buried at Westview. But Hal Hentz partnered with both. Hentz was born in Florida and was graduated from Emory University in 1904. He and Reid studied architecture together at Columbia University and at L'Ecole des Beaux-Arts in Paris.

Frederick Wakefield Patterson, 1882-1972, Section 5. Son of H. M. Patterson, Fred Patterson was summoned to Warm Springs, Georgia, 12 April 1945, to embalm the remains of President Franklin Delano Roosevelt, who died from a stroke while visiting at his retreat, the "Little White House." Patterson left Atlanta with two coffins for Roosevelt's widow Eleanor to choose between, and he modified the state car of the funeral train to accommodate the body and accompanying honor guard as it traveled to Washington, D. C., for the funeral. Robert Klara's *FDR's Funeral Train* tells the story. Photograph by Robert Parks.

Emily Stewart Harrison, 1874-1973, Section 4. Miss Harrison remembered enjoying the forested property she grew up with, an area that was being developed as the Druid Hills neighborhood. She donated the land to be maintained as forest. Her legacy, the Fernbank Forest, consists of 65 undeveloped acres, just off Ponce de Leon Avenue.

Administration building, 1975. The main cemetery office building was designed by Henry Howard Smith. It contains a reception area, family room, offices, and storage space for cemetery records and archives.

Richard H. Rich, 1901-1975, Section 5. Rich was the grandson of Morris Rich, who established a store on Whitehall Street (now Peachtree) soon after the Civil War. His brothers soon joined as business partners. Dick Rich was the son of Morris Rich's daughter Rosalind Rich Rosenheim. He changed his surname to Rich at the family's request, and served as president of the company from 1949 to 1976. Photograph by Robert Parks.

Phoenix Rising from the Ashes, Woodruff Park. The Rich Foundation donated this bronze statue by Jim Seigler and Gamba Quirino to the City of Atlanta in 1969. It was moved to its current location and rededicated at the time of the Centennial Olympic Games in 1996.

Florence Adeline Stephenson Candler, 1895-1977, Section 2. Florence Candler was the second wife of Asa Griggs Candler, Jr. She had served as his secretary for nine years when his first wife died, and they were married several months after that. She kept an office at Westview during the cemetery's Candler era, managing the cemetery, and its Abbey chapel was named in her honor. It was her decision to bury Asa Griggs Candler, Jr., beside his first wife rather than in the double sarcophagus intended for them in the Abbey. The sarcophagus is effectively a cenotaph for the Candlers today; Martha Powers recalls Mrs. Candler's wish that it never be used. See page 154. Photograph by Robert Parks.

Abbey, chapel doorway, 1945. The decoration over the entrance to the chapel features Florence Candler's initials, FC.

Frank Coll Bowen, 1905-1977, Section C. Bowen, along with other businessmen, purchased Westview in 1952. Previously he had worked in construction, including the building of Patterson and Son Spring Hill Chapel. Through that association, he became involved in other aspects of the cemetery business, particularly the Wilbert Burial Vault Company. Photograph by Traci Rylands.

William DeVaughn Lucas, 1936-1979, Sermon on the Mount Section. Bill Lucas was director of player development for the Atlanta Braves, the first African American to hold an executive position with a Major League team. Photograph by Traci Rylands.

W. Frank Gordy, Sr., 1904-1983, Abbey. Gordy founded the Varsity, the landmark drive-in restaurant on North Avenue near Georgia Tech. "What'll you have?" is the call-out for an order at the Varsity, and one of Atlanta's favorite sayings.

Varsity, North Avenue. The largest drive-in the country is a staple for Georgia Tech students and others. It was founded by Frank Gordy in 1946. Visitors have included President Bill Clinton, who was teased for his eating habits. Photograph by William Candler Bayne.

Robert Winship Woodruff, 1889-1985, Section 1A. Woodruff was only 33 years old when his father Ernest named him president of the Coca-Cola Company, two years after the elder Woodruff bought the company. He served as president for 30 years, and his power was inestimable, in terms both of political influence and philanthropy. He was "the boss" of Atlanta until he died in 1985.

Robert Woodruff statue, Woodruff Arts Center, Peachtree Street. Because of his philanthropy, Woodruff earned the nickname "Mr. Anonymous." For the 1968 funeral of Dr. Martin Luther King, Jr., he offered Mayor Ivan Allen, Jr., a blank check: "Whatever you need will be taken care of." Woodruff had learned of King's assassination in the Oval Office, where he and former Governor Carl Sanders were meeting with President Lyndon Johnson.

Windcrofte, Tuxedo Park. The palatial home of Robert Woodruff in Buckhead was built in the 1930s. After Woodruff died, politician Guy Millner bought the house for his wife for a first anniversary gift. In 2013, the house was listed for sale for $8.9M. Today Atlanta has a Woodruff Arts Center, a Woodruff Park downtown, and Woodruff libraries at Emory and at Atlanta University Center.

Dorothy Alexander Moses, 1904-86, Section 1. Alexander, a graduate of Atlanta Normal Training School and Oglethorpe College, was a ballet dancer and choreographer. She founded Atlanta Ballet in 1929. It was the first regional ballet company in the country, and is now the oldest professional dance company in America in continuous operation. In 1933, she wrote and staged *Heirs of All the Ages*, using 3,000 performers.

Beverly Means DuBose, Jr., 1918-1986, Section A1. DuBose was president of the Atlanta Historical Society, now the Atlanta History Center, where his extensive collection of Civil War artifacts is displayed. His epitaph reads, "DO WHAT'S RIGHT." Photograph by Traci Rylands.

Bryan Morel "Bitsy" Grant, Jr., 1910-1986, Section 1. Nicknamed "Bitsy" because of his diminutive stature, Grant was a tennis star in the 1930s, ranked in the top ten nine times. He escorted Olivia de Havilland to the premiere of *Gone With the Wind* in 1939. He was graduated from the University of North Carolina and served in World War II. He was inducted into the International Tennis Hall of Fame in 1972. Grant's marker is second from left.

Frank Hawks Maier, Sr., 1908-1991, Section 1. Maier was a jeweler, head of the Maier and Berkele Jewelry Store. He was a member of the Capital City Club. Photograph by Traci Rylands.

Dillard Munford, 1918-1993, Section C. Munford, with a degree in mechanical engineering from Georgia Tech, founded a chain of Do-It-Yourself stores, with 46 stores. He was chairman of the Chamber of Commerce and a trustee of Morris Brown College. He wrote an editorial column that was published in 30 weekly Georgia newspapers. Photograph by Traci Rylands.

Charles Manley Brown, 1903-1995, Section B. Brown was a Georgia Tech graduate and a politician. He served as a Fulton County commissioner, state representative, and state senator, and ran for mayor three times. Charlie Brown Airport is named in his honor.

Alice J. Hawthorne, 1952-1996, Section 38. During an otherwise joyous and successful Centennial Olympic Games in Atlanta in 1996, a bomb exploded on the night of 27 July in a crowded area of Centennial Olympic Park. Alice Hawthorne, an Augusta native, was the only fatality, but 111 were injured. After years of investigation that included the suspicion of security guard Richard Jewell, who had reported the bomb to the police and tried to evacuate the area, Eric Robert Rudolph was convicted of the bombing, as well as of other bombing attacks on an abortion clinic in Sandy Springs, another in Birmingham, and at the Otherside Lounge, a lesbian bar on Piedmont Road. Photograph by Allie Rivenbark.

Rankin McEachern Smith, 1924-1997, Section B. Smith was chairman of the Life Insurance Company of Georgia, and the first owner of the Atlanta Falcons of the National Football League. Photograph by Traci Rylands.

Georgia Dome, 1992, Northside Dr. The Falcons shared Atlanta-Fulton County Stadium with the Braves until the Georgia Dome opened in 1992. In 2013, plans were approved to construct a new stadium with a retractable roof south of the current site, left in the photograph, from the Sundial.

Robert Lawson Shaw, 1916-1999, Section C. Shaw was conductor of the Atlanta Symphony and founder of the Robert Shaw Chorale. No less a figure than Arturo Toscanini proclaimed him, while still in his 20s, "the maestro I've been looking for," when Shaw conducted the chorus for performances of Beethoven's *Ninth Symphony* and Verdi's *Aida* in the 1940s. Shaw conducted the Atlanta Symphony Orchestra from 1967 to 1988.

Dinah Marks, 1944-1999, Section 31. Marks, known as Madam Bell, operated a fortune-telling salon on Cheshire Bridge Road for many years. She drowned in the swimming pool of the Ritz-Carlton, and her funeral procession included a horse-drawn hearse. The elaborate mourning ritual and religious imagery are characteristic practices of Roma people.

Cenotaph for Ivan Allen, Jr., 1911-2003, Section 5. Allen followed his father both in the office supply business and in the powerful position of president of the Chamber of Commerce. In 1961, Mayor William Hartsfield decided not to run for another term, and Allen was elected mayor in 1962. Allen navigated the desegregated reception to honor Martin Luther King, Jr., upon his winning the Nobel Peace Prize, a messy road closure to preserve segregated neighborhoods, and the funeral for King in 1968. Originally buried in Westview, his body was translated to Oakland after his widow died in 2008.

Turner Field, 1996. Allen trumpeted the arrival of Major League sports to Atlanta, the Falcons in 1965, and the Braves in 1966. The Braves played in Atlanta Fulton County Stadium until "the Ted," named for owner Ted Turner, was converted from the Olympic Stadium. Turner Field houses the Ivan Allen, Jr., Braves Museum and Hall of Fame. In 2013 the Braves announced that they would move to a new stadium complex in Cobb County. Photograph by William Candler Bayne.

Nathaniel Hawthorne Bronner, 1914-2003, Section 6. Dr. Bronner, with his brother Arthur and sister Emma, taught cosmetology at the Butler Street YMCA in 1947. Geared to an African-American audience, their products and shows are known worldwide. The Bronner Brothers International Hair Show has attracted Martin Luther King, Jr., Jackie Robinson, Dick Gregory, and Benjamin Mays as guest speakers. In 1967 the Hyatt Regency Hotel opened; it hosted the Bronner Brothers convention for 20 years. Featured in Chris Rock's 2009 documentary *Good Hair*, the annual Bronner Brothers International Hair Show is now held at the Georgia World Congress Center. Photograph by Traci Rylands.

Donald Lee Hollowell, 1917-2004, Section 6A. Hollowell was a Civil Rights attorney. He sued the University of Georgia to gain admission for African-American students, gained the release for Dr. Martin Luther King, Jr., in 1960 from Georgia State Prison, and served as regional director of the Equal Employment Opportunity Commission for 20 years. Donald Lee Hollowell Parkway in northwest Atlanta, formerly Bankhead Highway, is named for him. Photograph by Traci Rylands.

Anne Coppedge Carr, 1917-2005, Section A1. A gardener and bibliophile, Carr founded the Cherokee Garden Library at the Atlanta History Center, one of the premier gardening libraries in the country.

Joseph West Jones, 1912-2005, Section A1. Jones was a senior vice-president of the Coca-Cola Company, who served as chief of staff and executive assistant to Coca-Cola chairman Robert Woodruff. Woodruff called him his "most trusted business associate." He was chairman of the Woodruff Foundation. Woodruff's South Georgia plantation, Ichauway, is named the Jones Ecological Research Center in his honor. Photograph by Traci Rylands.

Vivian Juanita Malone Jones, 1942-2005, Section 70. Jones was the first African-American graduate of the University of Alabama. In 1963 her admission to the university had been blocked—physically—by Governor George Wallace; President John F. Kennedy federalized the Alabama National Guard that day, and, escorted by 100 guardsmen, Jones registered. The scene was depicted in the 1994 movie *Forrest Gump*. She was director of the Civil Rights division of the Environmental Protection Agency. In October 1996, she was awarded the Lurleen B. Wallace Award of Courage. Her brother-in-law, Eric Holder, became the first African-American attorney general of the United States in 2009.

Columbarium, 2005, Abbey. Responding to the increasing popularity of cremation, Westview constructed this modern columbarium in 2005 in the yard of the Abbey. It contains niches for the cremated remains (ashes or "cremains") of 360 people.

James Rawson Haverty, 1920-2007, Section 31. The grandson of J. J. Haverty, Rawson Haverty served as president of the Haverty Furniture Company from 1955 to 1984. His book, *Ain't the Roses Sweet: 137 Years in Atlanta*, with a title based on a Frank Lebby Stanton poem, details the history of the family and of the furniture company.

James V. Paschal, 1920-2008, Abbey. Paschal was a restaurateur. His restaurant, with a motel and nightclub near Atlanta University Center, figured prominently in the Civil Rights movement. Photograph by Christian Moreno.

Paschal's, 1959, Martin Luther King Dr. The restaurant was a meeting place for Civil Rights movement planners. The 1965 Selma-to-Montgomery, Alabama, march was planned here. Coretta Scott King compared its importance in the Civil Rights movement to Boston's Faneuil Hall's in the American Revolution. The building has been owned by Clark Atlanta University since 1996, and requires restoration. Paschal's restaurants operate on Northside Drive and at the airport.

William Austin Emerson, Jr., 1923-2009, Section A1. Emerson was a journalist, responsible for coverage of the Civil Rights era in the Southeast for *Newsweek*. He covered school integration battles, Ku Klux Klan activities, and the Montgomery bus boycott led by Martin Luther King, Jr. He was also editor-in-chief of the *Saturday Evening Post*, 1965-9. Later he taught journalism at the University of South Carolina. Photograph by Robert Parks.

Samuel Cooper Inman, 1927-2010, Section B. The name Inman is famous in the city, reflected in Inman Park and Inman Middle School. Inman was a fifth-generation Atlantan, and grew up in the Swan House, built by his grandfather, the estate now forming the campus of the Atlanta History Center. He had a distinguished career in the construction business, building highways, bridges, and airports across the Southeast. The epitaph comes from Shakespeare's *Julius Caesar*. Photograph by Robert Parks.

Howard W. Creecy, Jr., 1954-2011, Abbey. Creecy was a Morehouse College graduate and pastor of Olivet Baptist Church in Fayetteville. He was elected president of the Southern Christian Leadership Council in January 2011, and died a few months later. At his burial some mourners complained about the flags at the Confederate Veterans' monument. Photograph by Christian Moreno.

Rodney Mims Cook, Sr., 1924-2013, Abbey. A descendant of Mayor Livingston Mims, Cook was a city alderman and member of the Georgia legislature. He was the first Republican elected to the Georgia House of Representatives since Reconstruction. He ran for mayor in 1968, supported by Ivan Allen, Jr. His obsequies included a private service at Alexandra Park, his son's Buckhead farm, and a public funeral at the Millennium Gate, conducted by Dean Sam Candler of St. Philip's Cathedral. Photograph by Christian Moreno.

James Christopher Kelly, 1978-2013, Section 6A. Chris Kelly was a member of the rap duo Kris Kross. The duo was best known for their hit 1992 song, "Jump," which was No. 1 on the Billboard Hot 100 for eight weeks and certified double platinum as a single. Kris Kross was also noted for their fashion style, which consisted of wearing their clothing backwards. Photograph by Traci Rylands.

Ria Pell, 1968-2013, Section 70. Pell was a restaurateur, running a popular landmark cafe on Memorial Drive, Ria's Bluebird. She was active in the gay, lesbian, bisexual, and transgender community. The Saturday after her sudden death, her funeral began with a miles-long car procession from the restaurant to Westview. There, after readings and eulogies in the chapel, mourners walked behind a vintage hearse to the gravesite. Following the burial, there was a party back at the Bluebird, with food, drinks, music, and fireworks.

Conclusion

Thus ends this tour of Westview Cemetery. Since its establishment in 1884, it has become a choice burial place for more than 100,000 people, many of them famous for their contributions to the history of the city and the state.

At nearly 600 acres, the cemetery is the largest in the Southeast, and its Abbey Mausoleum is among the largest in the country. The antique gatehouse, water tower, and receiving tomb, all dating from the 1880s and '90s, are very old by Atlanta standards— destruction and rebuilding have been the usual practice since Sherman's March to the Sea.

The Westview property figured in the Civil War, its having been the site of the Battle of Ezra Church, 28 July 1864. Some evidence of the battle is still discernable, and the grave of a casualty of that fighting was moved to the cemetery in the 1960s.

Among the residents are former mayors, governors, senators, newspaper editors and writers, novelists, painters, poets, preachers, teachers, and lawyers. The most famous include Joel Chandler Harris, Henry Grady, Asa Candler, and Robert Woodruff.

The grounds reveal two distinct cemetery styles. The lawn park style is characterized by family lots, dominated by single large monuments with the family name, surrounded by individual small markers for specific graves. The memorial park style, which originated with Forest Lawn in Glendale, California, uses flush bronze markers, and appears to be an expanse of lawn, often with a single piece of statuary in each section, the artwork installed by the cemetery owners themselves.

In 130 years of its history, the ownership and management have been in the hands of three groups. For its first forty-six years, the manager was Edgar Poe McBurney, whose 30-foot obelisk stands in a triangular grassy island near Henry Grady's mausoleum and Asa Candler's draped obelisk. After McBurney retired and a brief period of ownership by members of the Adair family, the cemetery was owned for nearly 20 years by Asa Candler, Jr., the flamboyant second son of the Coca-Cola founder.

It was during Candler's tenure that the Abbey was constructed, the last and largest project of the esteemed community mausoleum builder Cecil E. Bryan. Candler also developed new sections of the property in the memorial park style. He also built a trophy room to house his collection, having taken up big game hunting after losing interest in his other hobbies, which included auto racing, flying, yachting, and zookeeping, among others.

Since 1952 the cemetery has been operated by three generations of the Bowen family. They have continued to develop the memorial park sections of the cemetery, adding statuary to the named sections. They added a new administration building, to replace the poorly constructed trophy room complex that had previously served that function. They also added a columbarium to house cremated remains, and have developed additional sections, both in the memorial park style and with upright monuments, as needed.

The cemetery operates as a non-profit corporation governed by a Board of Trustees, and has sufficient room to expand through the next century or more. Westview continues to provide varied but dignified services to the community and region.

The double sarcophagus was intended for Asa Griggs Candler, Jr. and his second wife, Florence. When he died, Mrs. Candler instead directed that he be buried beside his first wife in Section 2. She later stipulated that the sarcophagus should never be used. It is effectively a cenotaph monument to the Candlers. Photograph by David Naugle.

Afterword by Franklin Miller Garrett, 1987

WEST VIEW: An Atlanta Beauty Spot of Peaceful Repose[10]

The so-called elegant 1880's comprised a decade of rapid and substantial growth in Atlanta. It came to resemble a medium-sized city rather than a fair-sized town, as in earlier years. Indeed, by 1884, it had achieved a population of nearly 54,000.

The city administration for 1884, headed by Mayor John B. Goodwin and Mayor Pro-Tem Thomas G. Healey, presided over a solvent concern. The city treasurer's office showed a surplus of receipts over disbursements for 1883 of $34,355.61. Indeed, with total receipts that year of $991,918.20, Atlanta was about to become a million dollar a year enterprise.

Even so, it was still a one-cemetery city, excepting family graveyards and church burial grounds in the immediate vicinity. Oakland, known until 1876 simply as the "City Cemetery," was, by 1884, not full but hard to get into. No more lots were available by purchase from the city.

The need for a new and more spacious cemetery did not go unheeded. In the summer of 1884 a group of leading citizens applied to the superior court of Fulton County for a charter under the name of West View Cemetery Company. On June 28th the charter was granted to the petitioners, who were: L. P. Grant, Walker P. Inman, George W. Parrott, James R. Wiley, John Stephens, James F. Burke, Edgar P. McBurney, Benjamin J. Wilson, Thomas J. Hightower, A. P. Woodward, James W. English, Thomas N. Chase, Jacob Elsas, Rufus B. Bullock, Jacob Haas, H. I. Kimball, J. C. Bridges, C. J. Simmons, C. W. Francis, L. De Give, Willia E. Ragan, W. D. Luckie, L. Gholstin, Jack W. Johnson, Benjamin E. Crane, Thomas L. Langston, and Henry H. Cabaniss.

Original officers of the company were Thomas L. Langston, President; Thomas J. Hightower, Vice-President; E. P. McBurney, Secretary; Joseph T. Orme, Treasurer; and Robert J. Lowry, E. P. McBurney, John T. Pendleton, Thomas L. Langston, T. L. Hightower, Rufus T. Dorsey, Joseph T. Orme, William A. Russell, and J. Carroll Payne, Directors.

In selecting a site, every thought of future need was taken into consideration, and a tract, the nucleus of the present cemetery, was purchased for $25,000. This represented an average of $45 per acre for the original 577 acres. The site was described at the time as being "four miles from the city, north of West End, on the Green's Ferry Road." Only twenty years before, on June 28, 1864 [sic], part of the ground had run red with the blood of Confederate and Union soldiers during the hotly contested battle of Ezra Church. Just

---

[10] It is interesting that this essay doesn't include any African Americans, and not very many women. Garrett's history of Atlanta is largely the history of white men in Atlanta and its environs. The near invisibility of blacks and women in 2,000 pages of *Atlanta and Environs* is a known feature.

across Green's Ferry Road from what was to become the main gate to West View, stood, for many years, Fulton County's original almshouse.

Edgar P. McBurney, leading spirit in the development of West View, took a ride through the grounds with a *Constitution* reporter on August 5, 1884. He remarked, as with the scribe, he drove through the by-ways and hedges of the delightful place:

"For years and years this will be a park. We have land enough here to last Atlanta forever. This is a labor of love and not a money making scheme, and the men who have it in charge intend to give Atlanta a cemetery that will be the admiration of visitors and the pride of our citizens. In time there will be a million dollars' worth of monuments on this ground. In a few days we will have a fine landscape gardener here who will be permanently employed to lay out and beautify the place. The whole tract will be laid out in drives."

"What do you propose to pattern after?"

"Woodlawn, one of the newest and most beautiful cemeteries in New York. I tell you truly, this cemetery will not be surpassed by any."

The first interment in West View, on the afternoon of October 9, 1884, was described by the *Constitution*:

> The first burial in West View cemetery took place yesterday, Mrs. Haskins, wife of Mr. C. R. Haskins, being laid away in that beautiful new city of the dead, just as evening shadows were longest, and the red glare of the sun tinted the western sky. The procession started from Jackson Street, near the Boulevard, passed into Peachtree and thence out Whitehall past West End to West View. The lot selected by Mr. Haskins is situated on a beautiful knoll not far from the entrance, and in sight of the receiving vault now in process of construction. Certainly a more beautiful spot could not have been selected, and there, amid the deep silence of nature in a place yet fresh with the upturned soil of the engineer's work, surrounded by the saddened husband, family and friends, the preacher said the last sacred rites, spoke a solemn prayer, and the earth closed about the casket to be removed only on the great day of awakening for all. It was a touching occasion, this first burial in the new cemetery, and few eyes were dry as the cortege took up its return to the bustling city of the living, that nestles away in the distance on her hundred hills.

On December 24, 1884, shortly after the opening of West View, the General Assembly passed an Act, Section 1 of which reads as follows:

"That drunkenness, indecent or lewd conduct or behavior, disorderly conduct of any time, are hereby prohibited within West View Cemetery, in Fulton County, and within one-fourth of a mile of the same in any direction."

In its issue of May 1, 1889, *The Atlanta Journal*, commenting upon "Atlanta's Cemeteries," had the following to say about West View:

"On the 13th of October, 1884, a private corporation was formed, with Mr. E. P. McBurney at the head, which made a purchase of 577 acres of land lying without the western part of the city limits, to be used as a cemetery. The property lies three miles from the center of town and can be reached by three drives and a dummy (street car) line. . . ."

"The object of the corporation is to make the cemetery what Atlanta needs—a landscape park, in which may safely rest the dead.

"No fences will mar the beauty of the hills and valleys of West View, and the lots are marked off with squares of Georgia marble that are even with the ground. The lawns are sown with Bermuda grass that is closely cut and weeping birches, willows, elms and other rare trees are set out on the beds.

"On the highest point in the cemetery, by the side of a long line of well-preserved fortifications where the battle of the 28th of July was fought, is a large circular mound reserved for the bodies of the Confederate veterans. This hill will accommodate four hundred bodies.

"West View has what no other cemetery in the south has—a receiving tomb, which holds conveniently 108 bodies. This is a handsomely constructed vault of Georgia marble and brick in the side of a hill. Bodies can be kept safely in this vault for any length of time before burial.

"Mr. McBurney says the corporation intends making West View as near like Greenwood in Cincinnati as possible, as that cemetery is considered the handsomest in the United States.

"Up to date one hundred and three thousand dollars has been expended in beautifying the grounds, and they already show up very handsomely.

"Policemen are kept on the grounds all the time and no idlers nor persons wishing to make merry are allowed to enter and damage the graves or otherwise do injury to the place kept sacred for the dead.

"Many of the most prominent citizens of Atlanta have already purchased lots in West View, and they are kept in order by the corporation.

"Altogether West View is a very beautiful place."

Two of the oldest structures in the cemetery are the stone gate house facing Gordon Street, still standing and closed, but intact, and the receiving vault mentioned in the 1889 newspaper article just quoted. A marble tablet, which seals the entrance, is inscribed:

1888
WEST VIEW RECEIVING VAULT
BUILT IN 1888 WHEN THE CEMETERY WAS 4 YEARS OLD. DIMENSIONS:
LENGTH, 25 FEET; WIDTH: 30 FEET; HEIGHT, 18 FEET; NORMAL CAPACITY: 36.
UNTIL THE EARLY 20TH CENTURY, ROADS THROUGH THE CEMETERY WERE OFTEN
IMPASSABLE IN WINTER. WHEN ICE, SNOW AND MUD BOGGED DOWN THE HORSE-
DRAWN HEARSE, IT WAS HERE THAT THE CASKET WAS KEPT UNTIL WEATHER
PERMITTED INTERMENT. GREAT SERVICE TO THE COMMUNITY WAS RENDERED BY THIS
VAULT DURING THE WINTER OF 1917-1918 WHEN ATLANTA'S INFLUENZA EPIDEMIC
CLAIMED HUNDREDS OF LIVES. VICTIMS WERE BROUGHT HERE AWAITING BURIAL. THIS
VAULT WAS PERMANENTLY SEALED IN 1945 BECAUSE OF THE AVAILABILITY OF
THOUSANDS OF CRYPTS IN WEST VIEW ABBEY-MAUSOLEUM.

Another old structure in the cemetery and no longer in use is the water tower, built early in the present century. During the Candler ownership, beginning in 1934, the lower part of the water tower was used as a museum in which to house and display the numerous hunting trophies accumulated by Asa G. "Bud" Candler, Jr., an indefatigable big game hunter.

Writing in 1914, Lucian Lamar Knight, compiler of State Records and later founder of the Georgia State Department of Archives and History, commented, in his *Georgia Landmarks, Memorials, Landmarks and Legends*, concerning West View:

"West View, the modern cemetery of Atlanta, is located four miles from the center of the city in the Green's Ferry Road. It is controlled by a joint stock company, organized in 1884. The site is a beautiful one for the purpose, and the grounds have been highly improved. There are several hundred acres of land within the enclosure, and for years to come it is likely to be the city's favorite burial-ground, though other cemeteries have since been opened.

"Here, also, a handsome Confederate monument, surmounted by the statue of a private soldier, musket in hand, has been erected on one of the highest points, and there are many substantial and costly memorial stones. The cemetery contains a number of historic shrines, including the vault in which the ashes[11] of the illustrious Henry W. Grady are entombed.

"To the left of the main driveway, near the foot of the first hill, occupying a lot donated for the purpose by the corporation, is the grave of (Admiral) Dewey's flag lieutenant, who planned the battle of Manila Bay (1898) and hoisted the American flag above the Philippines. The handsome granite shaft, on which is designed a rope coiled and knotted in sailor fashion, emblematic of service on the high seas, is inscribed:

LIEUTENANT THOMAS M. BRUMBY, USN
Died December 17, 1899, aged forty-four years…"

The West View Cemetery Association continued in operation under founder Edgar P. McBurney until September 1930 when the Frank and Forrest Adair, Jr., family took over. Four years later, in January, 1934, Asa G. Candler, Jr., took control. This noted Atlanta family operated the cemetery until 1952, when the late Frank C. Bowen succeeded to the management. Mr. Bowen's son, Charles E. Bowen, became President in September 1974 and after Frank Bowen's death in 1977, Charles Bowen assumed his position as Chairman of the Board.

When the Bowens took charge in 1952, the corporate structure was changed, whereby West View was made a non-profit corporation and continues as such. Under the present [1987] structure, the Board of Trustees and Officers are:

Charles E. Bowen, Chairman and President
Frank C. Bowen, Jr., Vice-President, Treasurer, Trustee
Martha M. Powers, Secretary, Trustee
F. Coll Bowen, III, Trustee
Charles D. Hurt, Jr., Trustee
Charles E. Bowen, Jr., Trustee
Thomas C. Bowen, Trustee

In 1943, during the Candler regime, West View began construction of a community mausoleum, challenging the finest the masters of the past ever built. Indeed, the finished

---

[11] Figurative. Grady was not cremated.

product, containing space for 11,444 entombments, combines ancient splendor, sacred halls and reverent purpose. In the Narthex, four of the Lord's parables are vividly portrayed on canvas. There are 27 stained glass panels in this beautiful chapel depicting the life of Christ, from the nativity through the crucifixion, and the resurrection. West View Mausoleum is the largest structure of its kind ever built under one roof.

Through the years, until 1975, a couple of smallish rooms in the rock gate-house had served as office space and a repository for the West View records, complete from 1884.

Finally outgrown, the time had come for a new office and reception building in 1975. Designed by architect Henry Howard Smith and built by Marthame Sanders at a cost of $1,000,000, the attractive structure admirably serves every purpose for which it was designed. It is located a short distance inside the main Gordon Road entrance on the left.

More than a century has passed since Mrs. C. R. Haskins was laid to rest on a beautiful October afternoon upon a knoll in West View. Since then she has been joined by more than 83,000 others, rich and poor, prominent and obscure, young and old, as time continues its inexorable march.

One of the oldest birth-dates recorded on a tombstone in West View is 1795. It marks the resting place of Charner Humphries, who died April 4, 1855. He was the founder and proprietor of the famous Whitehall Tavern, nucleus of old West End. Two stories in height it stood at the present northeast intersection of Lee and Gordon Streets, then the Newnan and Sandtown Roads. Built in 1835, ante-dating Terminus, later Atlanta, by two years, it was destroyed shortly after the Civil War. Charner Humphries, along with his wife, who died in 1851, and several children, were buried in a family cemetery in an area just to the north of the tavern. Here they remained until November 12, 1890, when all were removed to West View. Their graves are substantially marked.

Among many noted Atlantans, resting in West View, are, with year of demise:

[alphabetized list of 300 people, six of them female, with brief biographies]

During the decades that have passed since the writer of this article recorded all of the tombstone inscriptions in West View in 1935 and 1936, many notable citizens have joined those gone before. Among them are:

[alphabetized list of 270 people, one of them female, with very brief biographies]

Many more names could be added to this list, for, indeed, as of February 1987 there had been a total of 83,136 interments at West View, representing a cross-section of Atlanta citizenry from its beginnings. Some, such as Meredith Collier and Charner Humphries, were moved to West View from ancient family cemeteries in the present Atlanta city limits.

It has been noted earlier in this writing that the Atlanta campaign of the Civil War encroached upon land later to become West View. This occurred a week after the battles of Peachtree Creek and Atlanta, on July 20 and July 22 respectively. The Union army, endeavoring to reach the railroad between East Point and Atlanta, precipitated the battle of

Ezra Church on July 28, 1864. The area later became known as Battle Hill and now includes Mozley Park and a large part of West View.

Following this battle and lasting through most of August military activity, including the battle of Utoy Creek, continued in what is now southwest Atlanta. Many casualties ensued, including Lieutenant Edward P. Clingman, who was badly wounded near the home of Dr. Joseph Hornsby in the Campbellton District of old Campbell, now Fulton County. Dr. Hornsby took the wounded soldier home. Clingman subsequently died and was buried by Dr. Hornsby nearby. Not long afterward, the Clingman family, learning that their relative was buried on the Hornsby place, caused a substantial stone marker to be erected over his grave. It bears the following inscription:

LIEUT. EDWARD PETER CLINGMAN, C. S. A.
SON OF DR. & MRS. HENRY PATILLO CLINGMAN
OF GOLDSBORO, N. C. BORN APRIL 23, 1842
KILLED IN BATTLE NEAR ATLANTA, GA.
APR. 23, 1864 WHILE LEADING HIS COMPANY E
3 ARK REGT. CAVALRY IN A CHARGE AGAINST
THE FEDERALS. ENTERED THE ARMY APR 1861.
"The eternal God is thy refuge and underneath
are the everlasting arms." Deut. 33:27

It will be noted that the death date of the young soldier as carved on the stone is April 23, 1864. The month is obviously in error as no Union troops were engaged in battle in the immediate Atlanta area until mid-July 1864. The correct date, most probably, is August 23, 1864.

At any rate, the remains of Lt. Clingman and the monument on the old Hornsby place were removed to West View on July 30, 1961 under the auspices of the Sons of the Confederacy and the cooperation of West View management. The marker was placed fittingly beside a short section of a breastwork dating from the Battle of Ezra Church on July 28, 1864.

Happily West View has ample room in which to grow and expand. As a matter of fact, only about 50 percent of the total acreage has been developed into sections and even in the developed sections thousands of spaces are available.

West View Cemetery is, indeed, one of the beauty spots of the Atlanta area. Indeed, a leisurely drive or walk along its curving drives, with its rolling hills and handsome monuments and mausolea tend to instill in the observer a feeling of peaceful repose.

Apparatus

Bibliography

Abrams, Ann Uhry. *Explosion at Orly*. Atlanta: Avion, 2002. Print.

---. *Formula for Fortune*. Atlanta: Iuniverse, 2012. Print.

Alderman, Edwin Anderson and Joel Chandler Harris, eds. *Library of Southern Literature*. Atlanta: Martin and Hoyt, 1909. Print.

Ariail, Donald L. *Ansley Park*. Charleston: Arcadia, 2013. Print.

"Atlanta, Georgia." *Encyclopedia of Southern Jewish Communities*. The Goldring/Woldenberg Institute of Southern Jewish Life. Web. 28 October 2013.

"Atlanta, Georgia." Influenza Encyclopedia: The American Influenza Epidemic of 1918-1919: A Digital Encyclopedia. Web. 27 November 2013.

"Atlanta Roots Lie Under Real Estate's Family Tree." *Atlanta Business Chronicle*, 10 May 2010. Web. 7 December 2013.

AtlantaTimeMachine.com. Web. 3 February 2014.

Bauman, Mark K. "Factionalism and Ethnic Politics in Atlanta: German Jews from the Civil War to the Progressive Era." Feldman, Glenn, ed. *Politics and Religion in the White South*. Frankfort: U P of Kentucky. Print.

Beckman, Edward F. *Woodlawn Remembers*. Utica, New York: North Country, 1988. Print.

The Bell House Records. Atlanta History Center. Web. 15 November 2013.

Bickley, R. Bruce. *Joel Chandler Harris*. Athens: U of Georgia P, 1987. Print.

Bisher, Furman and Celestine Sibley. *Atlanta's Half-Century*. Atlanta: Longstreet, 1997. Print.

Black, N. Peters. *Richard Peters, His Ancestors and Descendants*. 1904. Print.

Bryan, Cecil. "Mausoleums." *AACS* [American Society of Cemetery Superintendents]: *Proceedings of the 43rd Annual Convention, Los Angeles, CA, 3-6 September 1929*. International Cemetery, Cremation, and Funeral Association. Web. 13 February 2014.

"Bryan Grant, 'Bitsy.'" *International Tennis Hall of Fame and Museum*. Web. 23 October 2013.

Bryant, James C. *Capital City Club: The First One Hundred Years 1883-1983*. Atlanta: Capital City Club, 1992. Print.

Burns, Rebecca. *Atlanta Yesterday and Today*. Lincolnwood, Illinois: Publications International, 2010. Print.

---. *Burial for a King*. New York: Scribner, 2011. Print.

---. *Rage in the Gate City*. Cincinnati: Emmis, 2006. Print.

Butler, Tray. *Moon Atlanta*. Berkeley: Avalon, 2012. Print.

Candler, Asa G., Jr. "Self-Surrender." *These Found the Way: Thirteen Converts to Protestant Christianity*. Soper, David Wesley, ed. Philadelphia: Westminster, 1951: 53-62. Email from Asa G. Candler VI, 21 January 2014.

Catron-Sullivan, Staci and Susan Neill. *Women in Atlanta*. Atlanta History Center. Charleston: Arcadia, 2007. Print.

CecilEBryan.com. Web. 30 September 2013.

Ching, Francis D. K. *A Visual Dictionary of Architecture*. 2d ed. Hoboken, New Jersey: Wiley, 2012. Print.

ChristianScienceAtlanta.com. Web. 3 February 2104.

Clark, E. Y. *Illustrated History of Atlanta*. Atlanta: Cherokee, 1971. Print.

Clemmons, Jeff. *Rich's: A Southern Institution*. Charleston: History Press, 2012. Print.

Constantelos, Stephen. "Jim Bagby Sr." Society for American Baseball Research Baseball Biography Project. Web. 1 August 2014.

Cook, Rodney Mims, Jr. *Atlanta's Parks and Monuments*. Charleston: Arcadia, 2013. Print.

Cox, Jamie. "Confederate Flag Protest at Westview Cemetery." Cascade Patch. 12 August 2011. Web. 21 August 2014.

Craig, Robert M. *Atlanta Architecture: Art Deco to Modern Classic, 1929-1959*. Gretna, Louisiana: Pelican, 1995. Print.

---. *The Architecture of Francis Palmer Smith: Atlanta's Scholar-Architect*. Athens: U of Georgia P, 2012. Print.

Crane, Frank. *Community Mausoleums*. Chicago, Cecil E. Bryan, Inc., 1917. Web. 13 February 2014.

Danylchak, Erica. "Georgia Historic Landscape Survey: Westview Cemetery." Cherokee Garden Library, 11 September 2008. Collection of Westview Cemetery, Inc. Print.

"David Mayer Family (1815-1890) Papers, 1839-1946. Mss 145." Catalog description. The Bremen Jewish Heritage and Holocaust Museum. Web. 28 October 2013.

Davis, Ren and Helen. *Atlanta's Oakland Cemetery: An Illustrated History and Guide*. Athens: U of Georgia P, 2012. Print.

"Dillard Munford, 75, Founded a Chain of Stores." *New York Times*, 18 September 1993. Web. 18 August 2014.

"Dorothy Alexander." *Encyclopaedia Britannica*. Web. 4 June 2014.

Dowling, Elizabeth Meredith. *American Classicist: The Architecture of Philip Trammell Shutze*. New York: Rizzoli, 1989. Print.

Elfers, James. "Jim Bagby Jr." Society for American Baseball Research Baseball Biography Project. Web. 1 August 2014.

EmoryHistory.emory.edu. Web. 11 October 2013.

Eubanks, Steve. "J. Douglas Edgar had a wife, two kids and promising future, but his taste for other women ruined everything. Sound familiar?" *Golf*. 2 April 2010. Web. 14 October 2014.

Evans, Eli N. *The Provincials: A Personal History of Jews in the South*. Chapel Hill: U of North Carolina P, 2005. Print.

Faust, Drew Gilpin. *This Republic of Suffering*. New York: Knopf, 2008. Print.

"F. C. Bowen, R. B. Nelson Buy Westview Cemetery." *Atlanta Journal Constitution*, 23 March 1952:16-C. Print.

Ferris, Marcie Cohen and Mark I. Greenberg, eds. *Jewish Roots in Southern Soil: A New History*. Waltham, Massachusetts: Brandeis U P, 2006. Print.

Findagrave.com. Web. 29 September 2013.

Finch, Susan. "Visit Westview Cemetery: A Hidden Gem in Atlanta." About.com. Web. 9 September 2013.

Franklin, Barry M. "Progressivism and Curriculum Differentiation," Rury, John L., ed. *Urban Education in the United State: A Historical Reader*. New York: Palgrave Macmillan, 2005. Web. 30 August 2014.

Funderburke, Dick. "Gentry House." *Ponce Press* 24.1 (January 2014): 1. Print.

Garrett, Franklin. *Atlanta and Environs*. 2 vols. Athens: U of Georgia P, 1969. Print.

"Gentry-McClinton House." www.atlanta.gov. Web. 27 January 2013.

The Georgian Revival. Web. 25 September 2013.

Georgia Tech Library Descriptions, "Hentz, Reid and Adler Architectural Drawings Collection." Web. 23 October 2013.

Glenn, Wilbur Fisk. *A Life Sketch of Rev. and Mrs. Wilbur Fisk Glenn*. 1913. Web. 10 February 2014.

Golden, Harry. *Our Southern Landsmen*. New York: Putnam, 1974. Print.

Gourney, Isabelle et al. *AIA Guide to the Architecture of Atlanta*. Athens: U of Georgia P, 1996. Print.

Greene, Melissa Fay. *The Temple Bombing*. New York: Addison Wesley, 1996. Print.

Gwin, Yolande. *Yolande's Atlanta: From the Historical to the Hysterical*. Atlanta: Peachtree, 1983. Print.

Hairston, Julie. *Georgian Terrace Hotel*. Louisville: Butler, 2010. Print.

Hallum, A. V. "Ferdinand Phinizy Calhoun, M. D." *Transactions of the American Ophthalmological Association*, 63 (1965): 5-7. Web. 16 January 2014.

Hartle, Robert. *Atlanta's Druid Hills: A Brief History*. Charleston: History Press, 2008. Print.

Hauk, Gary S. and Sally Wolfe King, eds. *Where Courageous Inquiry Leads*. Atlanta: Emory U, 2010. Print.

Haverty, Rawson. *Ain't the Roses Sweet*. Atlanta: Rawson Haverty, 1989. Print.

Hertzberg, Steven. *Strangers Within the Gate City: The Jews of Atlanta 1845-1915*. Philadelphia: Jewish Publication Society, 1978. Print.

Historic Campus Architecture Project. Web. 10 October 2013.

"History of Atlanta Ballet." Web. 15 October 2014.

"History of the Confederate Veterans' Association," 1890. Collection of Westview Cemetery, Inc. Print.

"History of Georgia Power." Web. 9 December 2013.

Hobson-Pape, Karri and Lola Carlisle. *Virginia-Highland*. Charleston: Arcadia, 2011. Print.

"Inquest Will Decide Harman Death Causes." *Miami News*, 6 March 1926, 17. Web. 14 November 2013.

An Introduction to West View Abbey. 1943 pamphlet in Westview Cemetery subject file, Atlanta History Center. Print.

"Ivan Allen III, 60." *Princeton Alumni Weekly*. Web. 16 October 2013.

Jewish Virtual Library. Web. 28 October 2013.

Jolley, Harmon. "Munford's Served the Do-It-Yourself Home Owner." The Chattanoogan. 21 March 2009. Web. 25 August 2014.

Jones, Anne P. *A Light on Peachtree: A History of the Atlanta Woman's Club*. Atlanta: Mercer U P, 2012. Print.

Jones, Joseph West, 1912-2005. Finding aid, Emory University Manuscript, Archives, and Rare Book Library. Web. 18 August 2014.

Jones, Sharon Foster. *The Atlanta Exposition*. Charleston: Arcadia, 2010. Print.

---. *Atlanta's Ponce De Leon Avenue: A History*. Charleston: History Press, 2012. Print.

Kath, Laura. *Forest Lawn: The First 100 Years*. Glendale, California: Tropico P, 2006. Print.

Keister, Douglas. "A Brief History of the Community Mausoleum," *Douglas Keister Photography*. Web. 21 July 2014.

---. *Forever Dixie*. Salt Lake City: Gibbs Smith, 2008. Print.

---. *Stories in Stone*. Salt Lake City: Gibbs Smith, 2004. Print.

Kennedy, Thornton. "Westview Cemetery has a legacy all its own." 28 November 2012. Neighborhood Newspapers.com. Web. 9 September 2013.

"King-Spalding History." FundingUniverse.com. Web. 16 October 2013.

Klara, Robert. *FDR's Funeral Train*. NY: Palgrave McMillan, 2010. Print.

Knight, Lucian Lamar. "Robert Cotten Alston." *A Standard History of Georgia and Georgians*, v. 6. (NP: Lewis Publishing Co., 1917): 2965-6. Web. 15 October 2013.

Kruse, Kevin. *White Flight*. Princeton: Princeton U P, 2005. Print.

Kuhn, Clifford M. *Contesting the New South Order*. Chapel Hill: U of North Carolina P, 2001. Print.

---, et al. *Living Atlanta: An Oral History of the City, 1914-1948*. Atlanta: Atlanta Historical Society, 1990. Print.

Lands, LeeAnn. *The Culture of Property: Race, Class, and Housing Landscapes in Atlanta, 1880-1950*. Athens: U of Georgia P, 2009. Print.

Leavey, Jane D., ed. *Creating Community: The Jews of Atlanta From 1845 to the Present*. Atlanta: Atlanta Jewish Federation, 1994. Print.

LeeonFire, "Walking in Westview—At Peace with History," 16 February 2011. *Life Lived Out Loud*. Web. 21 July 2014.

Leferer, Harry G. and Michael C. Page, *Sacred Places: A Guide to the Civil Rights Sites in Atlanta, Georgia*. Macon: Mercer U P, 2008. Print.

Lineage Book – National Association of the Daughters of the American Revolution. Vol. 24. Harrisburg, Pennsylvania: Telegraph Printing Company, 1907. Web. 11 February 2014.

Lyon, Elizabeth A. *Atlanta Architecture: The Victorian Heritage, 1887-1918*. Atlanta: Atlanta Historical Society, 1986. Print.

"Many Streets Get New Names." *Atlanta Constitution*. 17 October 1903. Web. 20 November 2013.

Marr, Christine V. and Sharon Foster Jones. *Inman Park*. Charleston: Arcadia, 2008. Print.

Martin, Anya and Duana Callahan, "The Houses that Haunt Atlanta." *The Signal*. Atlanta, Georgia State University, 27 October 1987. Web. 11 December 2013.

Martin, Harold H. *Atlanta and Environs*, vol. 3. Athens: U of Georgia P, 1987. Print.

Martin, Sara Hines. *Walking Atlanta*. Guilford, Connecticut: Falcon, 2001. Print.

McKay, John. *It Happened in Atlanta*. Guilford, Connecticut: GPP, 2011. Print.

Mintz, Adam. "Is Coca-Cola Kosher? Rabbi Tobias Geffen and the History of American Orthodoxy." Medoff, Rafael, ed. *Rav Chesed: Essays in Honor of Rabbi Dr. Haskel Lookstein*, vol. 2. Jersey City: KTAV Publishing House, 2009: 75-90. Web 7 February 2014.

Mitchell, William Robert and Van Jones Martin. *Classic Atlanta: Landmarks of the Atlanta Spirit*. Savannah: Golden Coast, 1991. Print.

Morganstern, Madeline. "Should Confederate Flag Fly at an Atlanta Cemetery? Black Leaders Say 'No.'" The Blaze. 11 August 2011. Web. 21 August 2014.

Morrill, H. L., Jr. "Beautiful West View Now Open To Public; Hundreds Drive Daily Through The Grounds. *The City Builder*, July 1931: 15-6. Print.

Negri, Ed. *Herren's: An Atlanta Landmark, Past, Present, and Future*. Atlanta: Roswell Publishing, 2005. Print.

New Georgia Encyclopedia. Web. 25 October 2013.

O'Connell, David. *The Art and Life of Atlanta Artist Wilbur G. Kurtz*. Charleston: History Press, 2013. Print.

Orr, N. Lee. *Alfredo Barili and the Rise of Classical Music in Atlanta*. Atlanta: Scholars P, 1996. Print.

Ottley, James M. *Atlanta History for Cocktail Parties*. Atlanta: James M. Ottley, 2009. Print.

PoliticalGraveyard.com. Web. 29 September 2013.

Pomerantz, Gary M. *The Devil's Tickets*. New York: Crown, 2009. Print.

---. *Where Peachtree Meets Sweet Auburn*. New York: Scribner, 1996. Print.

Powell, Lewis IV. "The Great Necropolis—Atlanta's Westview Cemetery." 24 December 2011. Southerntaphophile.blogspot.com. Web. 9 September 2013.

Ramos, Rachel Tobin, "New Life for Downtown Macy's Building." *Atlanta Journal Constitution*, 13 August 2009. Web. 9 October 2013.

Reed, Merl E. *Educating the Urban New South: Atlanta and the Rise of Georgia State University 1913-1969*. Macon: Mercer U P, 2009. Print.

Reese, Krista, "Brumby Family." New Georgia Encyclopedia. Web. 21 June 2014.

"The Re-interment and Funeral for First Lieutenant Edward Peter Clingman, CSA. . . ." Collection of Westview Cemetery, Inc. Print.

Roth, Darlene R. *Matronage: Patterns in Women's Organizations, Atlanta, Georgia, 1890-1940*. Carlson, 1994. Print.

--- and Andy Ambrose. *Metropolitan Frontiers: A Short History of Atlanta*. Atlanta: Longstreet Press, 1996. Print.

--- and Louise E. Shaw. *Atlanta Women From Myth to Modern Times*. Atlanta: Atlanta Historical Society, 1980. Print.

Rules and Regulations West View Cemetery Association. 1890 pamphlet in Westview Cemetery subject file, Atlanta History Center. Print.

Rylands, Traci Muller. *Adventures in Cemetery Hopping*. Web. 29 September 2013.

"Samuel Inman," *Atlanta Journal Constitution*, 25 August 2010. Legacy.com. Web. 4 September 2014.

Scaife, William R. *The Campaign for Atlanta*. Atlanta, William Scaife, 1985. Print.

Seibert, David. "Medora Field Perkerson: Author – Newspaper Columnist." The Historical Marker Database. Web. 1 August 2014.

Shadows of Paradise. Undated pamphlet in Westview Cemetery subject file, Atlanta History Center. Print.

Shankman, Arnold. "Atlanta Jewry—1900-1930." *American Jewish Archives*, November 1973: 131-155. Web. 7 February 2014.

Shannon, Margaret. "Candler Sells Cemetery Here." [*Atlanta Journal* or *Atlanta Constitution*], clipping in Westview Cemetery subject file, Atlanta History Center, N. D. (c. 10 January 1951). Print.

Shavin, Norman and Bruce Galphin. *Atlanta: Triumph of a People*. Atlanta: Capricorn, 1985. Print.

Shaw, Michelle E. "Ed Negri, 91; Former Herren's Owner." *Atlanta Journal Constitution*, 2 May 2013. Web. 15 October 2013.

Smith, William Rawson. *Villa Clare: The Purposeful Life and Timeless Art Collection of J. J. Haverty*. Macon: Mercer UP, 2006. Print.

Suddeth, Ruth Elgion, ed. *An Atlanta Argosy: An Anthology of Atlanta Poetry*. Atlanta: Franklin Printing Company, 1938. Web. 12 February 2014.

Sugar Magnolia Bed and Breakfast. Web. 3 February 2014.

Sweeney, Kate. *American Afterlife: Encounters in the Customs of Mourning*. Athens: U of Georgia P, 2014. Print.

Taliaferro, Tevi. *Historic Oakland Cemetery*. Charleston, Arcadia, 2001. Print.

TheatreOrgans.com. Web. 27 November 2013.

TheatricalOutfit.org. Web. 11 October 2013.

"Tullie Vilenah Smith." Tomotronics.com. Web. 2 January 2014.

Ufflelman, Louise, "Taking the High Road." Washington and Lee University News and Media Blog, 13 October 2014. Web. 28 November 2014.

Wells, Jeffrcy C. *In Atlanta or in Hell*. Charleston: History Press, 2009. Print.

"Westview Confederate Memorial Dedication April 22, 1990." Collection of Westview Cemetery, Inc. Print.

"West View's New Owners Plan Improvements." *Atlanta Constitution*. 10 January 1951. Print.

WilburnHouse.com. Web. 24 September 2013.

Williford, William Bailey. *Peachtree Street, Atlanta*. Athens: U of Georgia P, 1962. Print.

Wilson, Mrs. Henry Lumpkin, ed. *The Atlanta Exposition Cookbook*. Athens: U of Georgia P, 2012. Print.

Wikipedia.com. Web. 29 September 2013.

YaarabShrine.net. Web. 9 October 2013.

Photograph by Cindy Julian.

Alphabetical List of Graves

Joseph West Jones, 147
Vivian Juanita Malone Jones, 147
James Christopher Kelly, 152
James Lee Key, 87
George Edward King, 77
Wilbur George Kurtz, 123
Thomas L. Langston, 42
Thomas Warner Latham, 29
Enrico Leide, 126
Lucy Beall Candler Owens Heinz Leide, 122
William DeVaughn Lucas, 135
William Lycett, 40
Frank Hawks Maier, Sr., 140
Dinah Marks, 143
David Mayer, 25
Elisa A. Mayer, 25
Edgar Poe McBurney, 89
Ralph Emerson McGill, 125
Livingston Mims, 35
Sue Harper Mims, 44
Arthur Montgomery, 90
Dorothy Alexander Moses, 138
Dillard Munford, 140
George E. Murphy, 58
George Muse, 48
Guido Negri, 91
Cleland Kinloch Nelson, 47
Frances Newman, 60
Samuel Dexter Niles, 37
Benjamin Robert Padgett, 49
Oscar Pappenheimer, 49
James V. Paschal, 149
Frederick Wakefield Patterson, 131
Hyatt Meshach Patterson, 52
Ezzell Neal Pattillo, 127
Frederic John Paxon, 88
William Henry Peck, 26
Ria Pell, 152
Pellegrino Pellegrini, 43
Medora Field Perkerson, 119
Kate Lindsay Peters, 21

Geoffry Lloyd Preacher, 130
Isaac Newton Ragsdale, 80
Mary Millen Wadley Raoul, 79
Margaret Alston Refoule, 107
Joseph Regenstein, 103
Amos Giles Rhodes, 61
Richard H. Rich, 133
Walter H. Rich, 108
Zella E. Richardson, 104
Frank Mason Robinson, 53
Louise Phinizy Calhoun Robinson, 120
Roby Robinson, 120
Luther Zeigler Rosser, 54
Deryl E. Horsey Sharp, 126
Robert Lawson Shaw, 143
Charles Augustus Sheldon, Jr., 113
Family Sisson, 20
Francis Palmer Smith, 129
John Morton Smith, 45
Rankin McEachern Smith, 142
Tullie Vilenah Smith, 124
Lucile King Thomas Smith, 110
Jack Johnson Spalding, 82
Daniel Norwood Speer, 26
Frank Lebby Stanton, 59
Nan Bagby Stephens, 104
Josiah Percival Stevens, 64
Harry C. Stockdell, 43
Emma Mims Thompson, 40
Ida E. Thompson, 36
Charles Davis Tillman, 100
Dorothy Rogers Tilly, 127
Auguste Paul Tripod, 28
Henry Holcombe Tucker, 23
Cora Best Taylor Williams, 55
Jesse Parker Williams, 45
Grace S. Winecoff, 105
William Fleming Winecoff, 105
Ernest Woodruff, 101
Robert Winship Woodruff, 137
Matsotaro Yoshinuma, 72

Index

Photograph by Gary Adams.

ABOUT THE AUTHOR: Tennessee native John Soward Bayne is a mathematician, a graduate of Clemson University. He works as a senior consultant with AT&T Consulting, and lives in Atlanta's Old Fourth Ward neighborhood. This book grew out of papers delivered at the national meetings of the Cemeteries and Gravemarkers area of the American Culture Association. Clemson University Digital Press published his book, *Gravely Concerned: Southern Writers' Graves*, in 2010. His articles have appeared in *Eudora Welty Newsletter, Eudora Welty Review, Firsts, Studies in American Culture, Journal of the Georgia Philological Association,* and *Proceedings of the Mississippi Philological Association.* Selfie in Westview 24 November 2013, no relation.